MW01223709

Visions of Heaven

FOR

THE LIFE ON EARTH.

BY

ROBERT M. PATTERSON,

AUTHOR OF "PARADISE. THE PLACE AND STATE OF SAVED SOULS
BETWEEN DEATH AND THE RESURRECTION," ETC.

———

PHILADELPHIA:
PRESBYTERIAN BOARD OF PUBLICATION,
No. 1334 CHESTNUT STREET.

CONTENTS.

II.

III.

VI.

VII.

NOTE.

A RELATION exists between this volume and the one entitled *Paradise: The Place and State of Saved Souls between Death and the Resurrection*, previously issued by the Presbyterian Board of Publication. Each work is complete in itself, and not connected organically with the other. But, a few of the topics which were touched upon in the former publication are herein exhibited more at length, and each will be more instructive and comforting if read in the light of the other.

VISIONS OF HEAVEN.

PROLOGUE.

IMPORTANT PRINCIPLES.

WHAT do we really know concerning the life of heaven? And of what practical use is the knowledge?

These questions are often asked in a tone which expresses great skepticism as to the reliability of anything that may be advanced on the subject, and a conviction that the "speculations" which are indulged in can have no substantial influence on our conduct.

But God's inspired book glows with visions of the glorious world, and the light of it shines upon earth to guide us safely and happily over the path that leads to it.

In the following pages I endeavor to turn some

of the rays of that light upon our daily Christian course.

An underlying and pervading principle of the volume is that the gracious life of the redeemed on earth and their glorious life in heaven are essentially one: "Behold, the kingdom of God is within you." Luke xvii. 21.*

Speaking of the resurrection body, Dr. Charles Hodge has a paragraph which involves this truth, while it takes a wider sweep: "We know that every man has here his individual character— peculiarities mental and emotional which distinguish him from every other man. We know that his body by its expression, air and carriage more or less clearly reveals his character. This revelation of the inward by the outward will probably be more exact and informing in heaven than it can be here on earth. How should we know Peter or John in heaven, if there were not something in their appearance or bearing corresponding to the image of themselves impressed by their writings on the minds of all their readers?" †

---

* "Sanctification is glory in embryo; glory is sanctification come to the birth."—*Alford.*

† *Systematic Theology,* iii. 781.

The doctrine with which Isaac Taylor commences his *Physical Theory of Another Life* must, I think, be admitted: "If it be true that human nature, in its present form, is only the rudiment of a more extended and desirable mode of existence, we can hardly do otherwise than assume that the future being must lie so involved in our present constitution as to be discernible therein; and that a careful examination of this structure, both bodily and mental, with a view to the supposed reconstruction of the whole, will furnish some means of conjecturing what that future life will be, at least as to its principal elements." And in my investigation of the revelations of the inspired word on this subject I have had copious illustrations of his remark, that "it is not until the mind has been quickened by an intelligent curiosity, and has obtained also more than one clue to inquiry by the aid of hypothesis, that the actual extent to which the unseen world is open to us in the Scriptures comes to be suspected or understood." This book of Isaac Taylor is very fruitful of suggestions for the thoughtful; but it is marred by the two errors which pervade many works on the subject. It is inordinately hypothetical, dealing too much in suppositions and

too little with Bible revelations. And while
the author does not fail to see that the inspired
Book "directs us to look forward to a future
and distant epoch as the destined day in which
human nature is to put on corporeal incorrupti-
bility," yet he thinks of the state of the soul
between the death of the body and that future
day as one "not of unconsciousness indeed, but
of comparative inaction or of suspended energy,"
"a transition state, during the continuance of
which the passive faculties of our nature, rather
than the active, are to be awake"—a " state of inaction " and of " seclusion, involving, not improb-
ably, an unconsciousness of the passage of time "
in a body of some kind, though " impalpable and
invisible," and " of a more attenuated corporeity
than shall befit its ultimate condition of full
energy and activity." *

* Taylor's error flows from his adoption of the sheer metaphysical assumption that a body is necessary to enable a mind to
exist in space. An unembodied spirit, he assumes, is nowhere,
and can have no relation to the visible and extended universe,—
a position which only puts his difficulty back another stage,
while if carried out it is destructive of the scriptural doctrine
of God. It is this error which, in minds less reverential and
balanced than Taylor's, has led to the production of works on the
heavenly life that are offensive to the spiritual taste.

On the contrary, without permitting any speculation to interfere with the manifest teachings of
revelation, I hold that the human soul, when it
leaves the weakened and disordered body in death,
enters as a pure spirit upon a wider sphere of
action, and exerts its energies more freely than it
did here; and when, in the resurrection, it shall
reassume its physical frame as the spiritual body,
that body will be pre-eminently adapted to the
increased power to which the incorporeated spirit
has attained. And, I am very strongly inclined
to think, it not unfrequently happens that God's
people have indications of this increased energy,
as continuing through death, in a wonderful quick-
ening of their souls while their bodies are wasting
away, by which their spiritual vision glances
into the glorious world even before they are
called to it; as Waller has written:

> " The soul's dark cottage, battered and decayed,
>   Lets in new light through chinks that time hath made;
>   Stronger by weakness, wiser men become
>   As they draw near to their eternal home;
>   *Leaving the old, both worlds at once they view*
>   Who stand upon the threshold of the new."

The great change which passes upon saved
souls when they are translated from their earthly

tabernacles to the presence of the glorified Jesus
is their complete deliverance from sin and from all
the effects of sin, with, it may be, an enlargement
of powers which we cannot formulate in thought.
Our bodies shall rise from their graves essentially
the same that they are now, though gloriously
transformed and freed from everything that is
corrupting, weakening and cramping. Whatever
belongs necessarily to the spiritual life here shall,
perfectly dissociated from sin, belong to it hereafter; and whatever is revealed through the
inspired pages as the glorious life should be
striven after here.

" Although its features fade in light of unimagined bliss,
  We have shadowy revealings of the better world in this.

    A little glimpse, when Spring unveils her face and opes her
        eyes,
    Of the sleeping beauty in the soul that wakes in Paradise!

    A little drop of Heaven in each diamond of the shower,
    A breath of the Eternal in the fragrance of each flower!

    A little low vibration in the warble of Night's bird
    Of the praises and the music that shall be hereafter heard!

    A little whisper in the leaves that clap their hands and try
    To glad the heart of man and lift to heaven his thankful eye!

    A little semblance mirrored in old Ocean's smile or frown
    Of His vast glory who shall bow the heavens and come down

A little symbol shining through the worlds that move at rest
On invisible foundations of the broad almighty breast!

A little hint that stirs and thrills the wings we fold within,
And tells of that full heaven yonder which must *here* begin!

A little springlet welling from the fountain-head above,
That takes its earthly way to find the ocean of all love!

A little hidden likeness, all so faded and defiled,
Of the great, the good All-Father, in his poorest human
  child!

Although the best be lost in light of unimagined bliss,
We have shadowy revealings of the better world in this!" *

Each influences the other. The divine revelations of the future, apprehended by an active faith,
inspire and fashion the Christian life of the present : the life here, as it is formed and developed by
the grace of God, projects itself into the hereafter.

"The day which we falsely dread as our last is
indeed the day of our better nativity. We are
maturing on earth for heaven ; and even on earth,
in those noble studies which seem so little pro-
portioned to the wants of this petty scene, and
suited rather to that state of freedom in which we
may conceive our spirit to exist when delivered
from the bodily fetters which confine it to so

* *Sunday Magazine,* i. 281.

2

small a part of this narrow globe, there are pres-
ages of the diviner delights that await us—marks
of that noble origin from which the spirit was
derived." *

Endeavoring to read some of God's revelations
of the invisible, and the directions and examples
of his word for the growth of the true life in the
visible, I proceed in this volume on the following
method :

I. Taking the vision which was granted to the
apostle John at the commencement of his prophetic revelations, I exhibit, in the symbolic
teachings of the rainbow around the throne, some

---

* Dr. Thomas Brown's *Lectures on the Philosophy of the
Mind*, Lect. 97. " All the evil to which mortal men are liable
comes not from death, but from life, and if in dying they have the
soul sustained by Christian grace, death is to them not the night
of darkness in which a good life ends, but the dawn in which a
better life commences."—*Augustine*, Epistle cli. And Tennyson
has written, on a superficial view, the contrary, but really the
same :

> " Whatever crazy sorrow saith,
>   No life that breathes with human breath
>   Has ever truly longed for death.

> " 'Tis LIFE, whereof our nerves are scant,
>   O life, not death, for which we pant;
>   More life and fuller, that I want."

of the important principles of Christ's redeeming work, his preservation of the redeemed through the troubles of this world, and the rest to which he finally introduces them;

II. Passing to the closing vision with which John was favored, I evolve the scriptural teachings concerning the number of the redeemed—the incalculable multitude who are embraced in the redemption which the glorified Lord is administering. The latter part of this topic leads to the great act by which the hearers of the gospel receive the divinely-provided salvation, and to the pervading tone of the Christian life;

Following this, and considering the religious walk that is entered upon by the regenerate believer, I present—

III. The *devotional* element of piety, as suggested by our Redeemer's transfiguration;

IV. Connected with the same scene, the *social* feature of religion, as involved in the truth of the recognition of friends in heaven;

V. The discipline of *affliction*, as having its peculiar influence in forming the Christian character and preparing for the consummated bliss of redemption;

VI. The *active* element of the Christian life, in

the light of the different degrees of the heavenly reward;

VII. The *æsthetic* feature, as necessary to the full development of the soul for its religious life in this world, and for the highest enjoyment of the beautiful country.

The tendency of weak regenerate human nature is toward the cultivation of some one side of the Christian character, to the greater or less neglect of its other aspects. Thus there is too often exhibited a partial and a malformed piety.

"All of us, in religion as in intellectual culture, are in danger of being one-sided. Yielding to natural temperament, we are apt, whilst cultivating certain departments of Christian thought and activity, to neglect others. The believer of a contemplative disposition, for instance, may shrink from taking his proper share of exertion in the Church's work; whilst another Christian, strenuous in labor, may forget to some extent that the tree of piety can bring forth fruit to perfection only when watered with the dews of the Spirit through prayer and quiet communion Thus, the new man has deformities, growing inharmoniously, without fitting proportion of parts. And there are some elements of holy character which can be acquired only in trouble. The beautiful graces of resignation and sympathy can grow only in a soil through which has passed the ploughshare of affliction, and which has been watered by the rain of tears." *

On the other hand, some of the most injurious attacks upon Christianity are made by the presentation of the moral and the active elements of religion out of connection with the meditative and devotional, or, worse still, in their effect especially on the working classes, by arraying the contemplation of Nature and the worship of God therein, in antagonism to the higher remedial and

---

* " *Lectures, Exegetical and Practical, on the Epistle of James,* by the Rev. Robt. Johnstone, LL.B ," p. 76—one of the best critical and practical expositions to be found There is an important germ of truth in what some of the students of " *Comparative Theology* " push to the extreme of error And, on a wider scale, the corrupt religions of the world exhibit the weak tendency which shows itself in individuals and sects among Christians. Thus, James Freeman Clarke (in his " *Ten Great Religions,*" p. 21) says that under the influence of Brahmanism "the Hindoo mind is singularly pious, but also singularly immoral. . . . Gentle, devout, abstract, it is capable at once of the loftiest thoughts and the basest actions. It combines the most ascetic self-denials and abstraction from life with the most voluptuous self indulgence."

spiritual truths which the Creator has also revealed.

What God has joined together, however, none
should put asunder.   Sinless peculiarities of physical and mental constitution, which saving grace
does not change, will, it is true, run into the more
striking exhibition, in different classes, of particular features of our religion.   I suppose also that
even in the glorious land there will ever be differences in employments and in joys, caused by the
continuance of the various sinless characteristics
which prevail here—in some, for instance, intel-
lectuality, in others outward activity predominat-
ing—preferences existing too for particular lines
of observation, study, meditation, and for special
kinds of heavenly work   But we should all aim
after the most attainable harmonious combination
of the devotional, the social, the sympathetic, the
active and the beautifying elements of that life
which is produced here under the sanctifying influence of the Holy Spirit, and which, cultivated
here, develops into the complete and ecstatic life
of the hereafter.   .

I attempt no minute delineations of the life in
heaven.   I aim only to bring a few of the prominent revelations of it which are made in the Bible

to bear upon our daily course, and to exhibit in a free and practical way certain great features of the mode of existence here which is graciously connected with the state of glory. The heavenly life of earth, which is the preparation for the glorious life after death, is the predominant idea of these pages

There is a plan in the book binding into unity its various parts, but the form of presentation is not sharply systematic. Sometimes the descriptions of the life in glory predominate, and are left to make their own practical impression; at others the life on earth is pictured. The lines of the different visions also cross one another (being both independent of each other, and yet interdependent), as the various lines of our religion themselves do. The variety and the freeness which the Bible and the Christian life exhibit are thus imitated

I have endeavored to write for the masses of God's people, and have, therefore, not made obtrusive the critical machinery by which the truths of the volume have been evolved;* and, as a

* But perhaps the notes which I have scattered through the pages will suggest to students further reading on some of the topics

very cursory examination will at once discover,
the afflicted have occupied a prominent and
tender place in my mind during the preparation
of the work. I have remembered that the instructions of God's inspired servants largely deal
with his suffering children; and I have sought
to conform to his injunction, "Comfort ye, comfort ye my people. Speak ye comfortably to
Jerusalem, and cry unto her, that her warfare is
accomplished, that her iniquity is pardoned: for
she hath received of the Lord's hand double for
all her sins." Isa. xl. 1, 2.

One may do this without endorsing the extreme
assertion that "a life without pain would be a life
without love, for love is sympathy. Poetry is the
mirror of life. Well, suppose all the sorrow were
taken away from poetry, what would remain?
All true poetry is sad, for life is sad." * If that
were true, what about the life of heaven?
Plato's theory was that a state of pleasure is
always preceded by a state of pain. The assertion which I have quoted would not give even
the heaven of pleasure after earth's painful life.
But, in truth, prevalent as sin and sorrow are, the
gospel weaves the bright scarlet threads of joy

Luthardt's *Saving Truths of Christianity*, p. 43.

very thickly through the black warp of the world. Not only a calm and gently-toned peace, but the bliss of ecstasy, beams with its light and heat over the Christian course. "Come unto me," says the blessed Master, "all ye that labor and are heavy laden, and I will give you rest. Take my yoke upon you, and learn of me; for I am meek and lowly in heart: and ye shall find rest unto your souls: for my yoke is easy, and my burden is light." Matt. xi. 28–30. The apostle Paul, having complied with the gracious invitation, declares for himself and for all who imitate 'him: "Being justified by faith, we have peace with God through our Lord Jesus Christ: by whom also we have access by faith into this grace wherein we stand, and rejoice in hope of the glory of God. And not only so, but we glory in tribulations also: knowing that tribulation worketh patience; and patience, experience; and experience, hope; and hope maketh not ashamed; because the love of God is shed abroad in our hearts by the Holy Ghost which is given unto us." Rom v. 1–5. And, with an earnest repetition, the great doctrinal and practical writer of the New Testament, exhorts, " Rejoice in the Lord alway; and again I say, Rejoice." Phil iv. 4.

I.

THE RAINBOW IN HEAVEN: CHRIST'S REDEEMING WORK.

 DOOR in heaven was open to the apostle John. Rev. iv. i. He entered the brilliant place where Jesus Christ the exalted Saviour, the unfallen angels and the glorified redeemed are. He beheld the throne of Jehovah; for God is the great King of the universe, and heaven is the central place, the metropolitan city, the royal capital of his empire.

A sea of glass, like unto crystal, was before the throne, as, in the court of the Jewish temple, there was a brazen sea in which it was necessary for the priests to wash before offering sacrifices to God. The service of God is evermore a pure service. Those who shall participate in the ever-lasting worship of the upper sanctuary must have their souls cleansed from guilt and from defile-ment in the fountain which has been opened for sin and for uncleanness ; and that fountain is the blood of Jesus Christ, which cleanseth from all sin.

Round about the throne appeared the representatives of those who are purified in that fountain —four-and-twenty elders—the number drawn perhaps from the twelve tribes of the Old Testament Church and the twelve apostles of the New, thus embracing the whole Church of God under its two dispensations ; and the four living creatures,* representing man redeemed, glorified and perfected, from all quarters and nations, and fitted for heaven, though once cast out of Paradise. †

They united in the enrapturing worship of God— a worship which, while at this stage it addressed

* Not " beasts," as our version unhappily has it.

† Dr. Fairbairn has in his *Typology of Scripture* (Pt. ii. ch. i. sec. 3) an exhaustive examination of the import of the cherubim or living creatures as they appear in different parts of the Bible. His view is the one which I adopt, without exhibiting the reasons, though it is not perhaps the commonly-accepted one. Fausset, in his notes on Ezekiel i., presents it in this form : " The cherubim probably represent the ruling powers by which God acts in the natural and moral world. Hence they sometimes answer to the ministering angels ; elsewhere to the redeemed saints (the elect Church), through whom, as by the angels, God shall hereafter rule the world and proclaim the manifold wisdom of God."

the Most High as the Creator of all things, contains in the threefold ascription, "Holy, holy,
holy, Lord God Almighty, which was, and is, and
is to come," no dim implication of the Trinity, of
the absolute God in the past, the redeeming
Christ of the ever-present, and the sanctifying
Spirit in the present and future application of
redemption's blessings.

This truth is rendered clearer in the description
as it is continued in the fifth chapter. It was the
purpose of God to reveal the history of the
Church in the world down to its everlasting glorification. That history was written in a volume
of seven rolls, each roll containing a separate
stage in the development of the Church, and
sealed with a separate seal, which had to be
broken before the record could be read. No man
could open those seals; God's purposes are secret
until he chooses to declare them, and all the revelations that he makes come through the redeeming Christ, his own beloved Son. The crucified
Lamb therefore appeared in the midst of the
throne and of the redeemed. While he is God,
he is also man, and he is for ever, even in heaven,
one with his people and among them. "For the
Lamb which is in the midst of the throne shall

feed them (or "tend" them as a shepherd his flock), and shall lead them unto living fountains of water." Rev. vii. 17. It is as the atoning sacrifice that he dwells with them in glory; and to them, while they are in a state of grace, he makes known the will of God through the written revelation. He was able to break the seals, and he directly exposed to the apostle, in his vision, the whole history that followed.

As the glorified Redeemer appeared to take the book, the redeemed worshiped him with a song different from that of creation, which had been addressed immediately to the absolute One upon his throne. They had learned the new song of redemption, because he had redeemed them from sin and from wrath. "Thou wast slain, and hast redeemed us to God by thy blood out of every kindred, and tongue, and people, and nation; and hast made us unto our God kings and priests; and we shall reign on the earth."

Then was heard still another song in which other voices joined. The holy angels united with the redeemed. They cannot say, "Thou hast redeemed *us* to God by thy blood." Pure and exalted as they are, the Son of God is not as near to them as he is to the vilest human

sinners who are saved by grace; for "he took
not on him the nature of angels, but he took on
him the seed of Abraham." Heb. ii. 16.* But
though they cannot join in the song of redemption, they can, with redeemed men, cry out,
"Worthy is the Lamb that was slain, to receive
power, and riches, and wisdom, and strength, and
honor, and glory, and blessing."

The vision extending through these two chap-
ters is a thrilling one. It is freighted with the
richest truth. Having given a brief exhibition
of its general significancy, as was necessary for a
clear understanding of the rainbow around the
throne, I return especially to gaze upon this
feature of it.

THE RAINBOW.

Among natural objects the rainbow is one of
the most beautiful. Arching the clouds; rising

* Strictly, "He lays not hold on angels, but on Abraham's
seed he lays hold "—*i e.* to help them. But our version expresses
the full truth; for the way in which he took hold to help is
stated in v. 14: "As the children are partakers of flesh and blood,
he also himself likewise took part of the same." It is strange
that any readers of the Bible should suppose that the angels are
the glorified spirits of redeemed men, and that children should
be taught to want to be angels! That is too low an aspiration.
More than, and above, the angels we are to be!

from earth to heaven, and bending down from heaven to earth again; its form the strongest and most graceful of all geometrical figures; painted by the luminary of our skies in bright water-colors on the dark background of a storm-cloud that has rushed across the earth; "smiling on the faded storm;" caused by the sun, away in the west, shining through rain-drops as they fall away toward the east; its colors various and gently fading into each other,—there is scarcely anything in Nature that will so attract all ages and all conditions of men. "Look upon the rainbow " (exclaims the writer of the apocryphal book of Ecclesiasticus, amid a description of the glories of Nature, in ch. xliii. 11, 12), "and praise Him that made it; very beautiful it is in the brightness thereof. It compasseth the heaven about with a glorious circle, and the hands of the Most High have bended it." The child, in its mother's arms, claps its hands at the thing of beauty. The boy, in the hilarity of his young life, will talk of the gold that is at the foot of the arch. The man of science finds in it matters that baffle his powers of investigation. Ever new and ever young, the eye tires not of it. From season to season it is renewed for the delight of

every age. As we gaze upon it we can almost
sympathize with the feeling of the poet:

> " Triumphal arch, that fill'st the sky
>   When storms prepare to part !
> I ask not proud Philosophy
>   To teach me what thou art.
>
> " Still seem, as to my childhood's sight,
>   A midway station given
> For happy spirits to alight
>   Betwixt the earth and heaven.
>
> " Can all that optics teach unfold
>   Thy form to please me so,
> As when I dreamed of gems and gold
>   Hid in thy radiant brow ?
>
> " When Science from Creation's face
>   Enchantment's veil withdraws,
> What lovely visions yield their place
>   To cold material laws !"

But in this vision of heaven the bow derives
its chief significancy from its appointment by
God as a sign of the covenant of grace. After
the flood which destroyed the race with the ex-
ception of Noah and his family, God renewed
that covenant with the patriarch, and appointed
the sun-painting as a token of it. We can
scarcely be mistaken in supposing that this sug-

gested the apocalyptic imagery; and like all the imagery of the book of Revelation it has a deep meaning.

If I am asked whether I believe that there is really a throne surrounded by a rainbow in the glorious place, I answer: From the necessity of the case, in dealing with creatures of sense any description which endeavors to bring before us the lofty spiritualities of eternity must be clothed in a sensible form to enable us to receive some adequate idea of the truths that it contains. Much of the drapery of these revelations is manifestly of a figurative cast. At the same time, it would not be irrational to suppose that such a scene may really be in the beautiful land Heaven is a place with natural scenery.* But

---

* I am exceedingly gratified to observe that in *Nature and the Bible*, published since my *Paradise* was issued, Principal Dawson of Montreal, writing predominantly from the side of science, presents the view of the locality of heaven which I have taken in that volume writing from the side of revelation. He says (pp. 69, 72): '' In the Bible the highest heaven is certainly a definite place. where God's presence is specially manifested, although at the same time it pervades the whole universe . . . It is beyond the limits of the visible universe, being the ' heaven of heavens,' and is tenanted by spiritual beings whose nature can be explained to us only in figures of speech. It is a place of special manifest-

whether it be literal or figurative, its deep spiritua
lessons are the same.

ation of God's power, but does not limit or contain his energy.
It is the centre whence spiritual messengers are despatched to
all parts of the universe.   Lastly, at the resurrection our bodies
are to take on the condition of heavenly or spiritual bodies, as
distinguished from natural, and the conditions of heaven are to
descend to earth and to be established therein, so that heaven
and earth become one in nature, and are permanently identified.
. . . Science and revelation, standing on the extreme verge of
their respective fields, both point to a mysterious centre of the
universe of God, whence emanate powers that extend to the
utmost limits of space, and where dwells glory inaccessible,
which eye hath not seen, neither hath it entered into the heart of
man to conceive.   Strauss has ventured to say that no man
'having a clear conception in harmony with the present stand-
point of astronomy can represent to himself a Deity throned in
heaven.'   On the contrary, astronomy itself leads us to the supposition that God, while, like his own great forces of gravitation
and heat, pervading and penetrating all things, may, like these
forces, exert his power from a grand dominant centre of creation,
where his throne may be in the same figurative sense in which
the earth is his footstool."   The 580th number of *The Spectator* is
a charming little lay essay by Addison on the subject, in a place
where it would not be looked for; I have happened to notice it
just as I send this to press.   And, says Charnock among some
of the compact sentences which mark his *Divine Attributes*,
"Heaven is the court of God's majestical presence, but not the
prison of his essence.   It is the richest, vastest, most steadfast
and majestic part of the visible creation."

THE SAFETY OF CHRIST'S PEOPLE.

1. The position of the symbol is suggestive. In the vision the first thing that the apostle noticed was the throne with the rainbow encircling it; * and it introduced a series of judgments upon ungodly men and nations, mingled with promises of grace to God's people, which, united in their fulfillment, were to result in the overthrow of all evil and the saving of the chosen ones for the full glory of heaven.

He that sat upon the throne was like a jasper and a sardine stone or cornelian. The jasper of the ancients was a resplendent and translucent stone. It may be emblematic of the perfect purity of the divine nature. The sardine is red. Its color may represent the awful punitive justice of God He is the infinitely holy and just One. In his dealings with sinners holiness and justice are the first attributes which shine forth from his throne.

While the apostle beheld, out of the throne proceeded lightnings and thunderings and voices. God is terrible to the unbelieving and impenitent,

---

* " A complete circle (type of God's perfection and eternity— not a half circle, as the earthly rainbow) surrounding the throne vertically."

and in his holiness and justice he is about to launch upon a world of sin punishments which, like the blasting effect of lightnings and the awful noise of thunderings, shall carry destruction wherever they go. He is coming forth as the God of judgment upon the earth. Woes are to be visited upon ungodly nations, and are to wind up in a conflagration of fire, after which the air of heaven shall be still, peaceful and calm, as the sins of the antediluvian world brought on a flood which destroyed the sinful race, though its cessation left the earth beautiful and productive to the saved family.

But surrounding the throne, rimming and tempering the holiness and the justice of the Most High, appears the bow, the sign of God's covenant of salvation. The holy and just One is administering his kingdom with reference to his gracious plan of redemption. Even his lightnings, his thunderings and his voices of wrath go forth, under that, to punish his enemies and to save his subjects. The judgments which are to be denounced through the rest of the book shall not harm his beloved people. They may flash *around* them—they flash against and destroy only their enemies. The Church and its individual

members may be called upon to go through trials
severe and long protracted, but in the end they
shall be brought unharmed out of them. They
may be cast into the furnace, but to be purified,
not destroyed.

God and his judgments within the bow of
promise, the security of his people, their sure preservation and deliverance,—this is the first great
teaching of this vision. Jesus is made Head over
all things to the Church for the purpose of bringing all its members to salvation. He lives and
rules over all men and all nations and all worlds,
to gather his elect in perfect safety from the four
winds, and to save them from all trials. The
government of the universe shall be administer-
ed so as to bring all the redeemed to heaven.
Every soul embraced within the covenant shall
be drawn into the ark of life and kept there.
Thus we have suggested the lesson which the
prophet Isaiah pointedly asserts in the fifty-fourth
chapter of his prophecy: "No weapon that is
formed against thee shall prosper; and every
tongue that shall rise against thee in judgment
thou shalt condemn."

The Church of Christ has the protection of
heaven's King. He that touches it, so as to

injure even its humblest members, insults the
Monarch of the universe, who will break in
pieces like a potsherd the persecutors of his
people, and bring his chosen in safety out of
every tribulation.

With a slightly different shading, and on a
narrower scale, this precious truth had been
symbolized to Ezekiel in the majestic vision that
moves across the brilliant panoramic word-painting of the first chapter of his prophecy. A cloud
of whirlwind and of fire rolled toward him. Its
centre was a terribly intense brightness. The
lightning incessantly blazed from and around it.
In it appeared the cherubim. Above them was
the firmament like dazzling crystal; and in it a
throne, "as the appearance of a sapphire," on
which was the Divine Man, with the glancing look
of polished brass. He was coming to vindicate
his holiness and justice by judgments upon Jerusalem and apostate Israel. But there was a gracious
glow around the storm-cloud and the throne, for
"as the appearance of the bow that is in the cloud
in the day of rain, so was the appearance of the
brightness round about. This was the appearance of the likeness of the glory of the Lord."
v. 28. "Amidst his fiery judgments on Jerusa-

lem he still looked on the bow and remembered his covenant with Israel, and therefore reserved mercy for the elect remnant. So in all ages, amidst his punitive visitations upon the reprobate he has never lost sight of his covenant of love to his believing people."

And again, in Rev. x., amid the woes that God is pouring out upon the world, the mighty angel who comes down from heaven, with control over sea and land, to proclaim that there shall be time no longer, and to inflict judgments too fearful to be made known, is "clothed with a cloud, and a rainbow upon his head, and his face as it were the sun, and his feet as pillars of fire." v. 1. Terrors unutterable, and more horrifying than the world has witnessed in the past, are yet to come upon the wicked, but the redeemed shall be preserved through them all.

HEAVEN A PLACE OF REST.

This assumes that, in connection with these judgments, God's people experience sufferings while on earth, for they are still in the world of sin, and mingled with those who are beneath God's wrath. But in contrast with this is the next great teaching of the vision.

2. Heaven is a place of rest at the close of earth's stormy day.

As Noah looked upon the rainbow when it first appeared after God's gracious promise to him, he could not fail to remember his surprising preservation. The sins that had so fearfully prevailed among his fellow-men; the grace which had kept him from falling into them; the messages of warning that for one hundred and twenty years he had been commissioned by God to proclaim, but which fell unheeded upon the ears of the hardened generation; the construction of the ark according to the divine command, though wicked scoffers mocked and taunted him for his supposed folly; the overspreading of the heavens with the portentous clouds; the slow and gradual falling of the rain; its persistent descent day after day, with the breaking up of the fountains of the great deep, while, at last, men in agony, ascending from one hilltop to another, tried to escape the surely approaching destroyer; the expansive waste of waters beneath which a world had been drowned, while he and his family alone were saved,— the events were all written on the clouds, and appeared most vividly on memory's page every time he looked upon the beautiful arch.

So through the rainbow and the throne the saved look from the heights of heaven upon the wonderful way of salvation by which God has led them. The fearful sins of this world; their own particular and individual transgressions; the wrath of God, its fierce premonitory flashings here, its full fire in the lower world; their deliverance from sin and from suffering through the atoning Saviour received by faith: every time they look up to the throne and gaze upon Him who appears still a Lamb as it had been slain, though now triumphant, the whole dark yet bright, frightful yet alluring, panorama must roll before their eye while they burst forth into a new song: "Thou wast slain, and hast redeemed us." Heaven remembers earth and its divine salvation. And very pleasant recollections there are, in heaven's memory, of the redemption received on earth.

As each soul enters the land of glory and gazes upon its brilliant scene, it must at once recall the hour when first it believed and enjoyed the consciousness of pardon and acceptance with God. That was a time of joyful calm after distress, and anxiety and fear. The weary hours of dread and terror through which souls so often pass under the convincing influence of the Holy

Spirit before relief comes! But how sweet the
rest when it is received! How delightful the
joy of salvation through a crucified Saviour seen
by faith, after the agony of unbelief and pungent
conviction! The remembrance of it must be one
great element in the happiness of heaven To
the glorified redeemed, as they look back upon
earth, the rainbow is the token of deliverance
from the wrath of God.

THE DIVINE LOVE IN TRIALS.

Moreover, the gorgeous sight is a reminder of
the divine love that appeared even in their earthly
trials.   Many a gust the people of God must pass
through in this world.   Troubles rain upon them
over their whole course.   But all the while there
is a bow on the clouds.   The glorified now gaze
upon it; and so shall we if we are faithful unto
death and receive a crown of righteousness.

" Some time, when all life's lessons have been learned,
      And sun and stars for evermore have set,
   The things which our weak judgment here have spurned,
      The things o'er which we grieved with lashes wet
   Will flash before us out of life's dark night,
      As stars shine most in deeper tints of blue;
   And we shall see how all God's plans were right,
      And how what seemed reproof was love most true

" And we shall see (while we frown and sigh
   God's plans go on as best for you and me)
How, when we called, he heeded not our cry,
   Because his wisdom to the end could see.
And e'en as prudent parents disallow
   Too much of sweet to craving babyhood,
So God, perhaps, is keeping from us now
   Life's sweetest things because it seemeth good.

" And if, sometimes, commingled with life's wine,
   We find the wormwood, and rebel and sink,
Be sure a wiser Hand than yours or mine
   Pours out this portion for our lips to drink
And if some friend we love is lying low
   Where human kisses cannot reach his face,
Oh, do not blame the loving Father so,
   But bear your sorrow with obedient grace.

" And you shall shortly know that lengthened breath
   Is not the sweetest gift God sends his friend,
And that sometimes the sable pall of death
   Conceals the fairest bloom his love can send.
If we could push ajar the gates of life,
   And stand within and all God's workings see,
We could interpret all this doubt and strife,
   And for each mystery could find a key.

" But not to-day.   Then be content, poor heart !
   God's plans, like lilies pure and white, unfold :
We must not tear the close-shut leaves apart—
   Time will reveal the calyxes of gold.

And if, through patient toil we reach the land
  Where tired feet, with sandals loose, may rest,
 When we shall clearly know and understand,
   I think that we will say that 'God knows best.'"

Behold the bow which in the summer evening so gracefully arches the eastern sky! It tells you that a storm has passed over the earth which has been of incalculable value to the parched land. The wind accompanying it may have torn up trees; the rain may have deluged streams and carried away property, and marred some pleasure of the day; but the air has been purified and cooled; the gentle zephyrs of health float over you; every raindrop that has fallen is worth its weight in gold in the world's great garner; for while the sun shines upon and through the drops as they fall, it shines also on the earth which receives them, and under their magic touch vegetable life bursts into new vigor.

So the storms of sorrow that fall upon the true people of God sometimes look black—how black and gloomy!—while they are in progress. To some things they are very antagonistic. They fiercely destroy the lust of the flesh, the lust of the eye and the pride of life. They carry away many a creature comfort on which we would lean for support. They flood many a source of joy that we would like to have, and drown many a scheme which we have marked out. But as the soul ascends to the blissful land, the bow appears, telling it at once not only that all its troubles are over and that rest is entered into, but that the storms themselves were means of blessing in rendering more fruitful the graces of the Christian life. If any of my readers who are the penitent followers of Jesus are passing through severe tribulations, let them remember that it was one of the most extreme representatives of the class who wrote—

> " Ye fearful saints, fresh courage take :
> The clouds ye so much dread
> Are big with mercy, and shall break
> In blessings on your head."

They shall be convinced of that when they gaze upon the rainbow-encircled throne. Strive to realize it now, and by Christian submission and grace receive the benefit of the clouds as they arise. " No chastening for the present seemeth to be joyous, but grievous ; nevertheless, afterward it yieldeth the peaceable fruit of righteousness unto them which are exercised thereby." Heb. xii. 11. If there were no clouds there could be no rainbow ; it is after a stormy conflict that souls look upon the rainbow of heaven.

TRIALS OF JESUS

It should most touchingly enforce the lesson of submission to remember that our ascended Saviour passed through such fearful troubles in working out our redemption, and that he is reminded of them by this brilliant scene in heaven. He continues to be God and man in two distinct natures and one person for ever. In this description both his natures are pointedly exhibited to us ; for while, as God, the throne which is encircled by the rainbow belongs to him in common with the Father and the Spirit, he is also in the midst of the elders, the representatives of the redeemed, and with them he looks on the glorious arch. It is the shining forth of the divine nature through that human form which paints the brilliant image.

Now, the apostle Paul declares that Jesus " for the joy that was set before him endured the cross, despising the shame, and is set down at the right hand of the throne of God." Heb. xii. 2. The human nature of the Redeemer, though strengthened and made sure for its work by its inseparable union with the divine, yet, under that, was supported, in his years of obedience and of suffering to the cruel death of the cross, by the assurance of the joy that was set before him in bringing home many sons unto glory; and in heaven he beholds the memorial of the sufferings and the reward.

A baseless legend represents his head while on earth as always encircled by a halo; a heavenly light he had to guide him through his afflictions, and now it shines most beautifully in the glorious land. The redeemed remember their deliverance from sin and from wrath; he forgets not the incidents of his earthly life through which that deliverance was secured. His pre-existence before all worlds and his birth in Bethlehem's manger, the cross of Calvary and the throne of heaven, are for ever and inseparably blended in his history and in his memory. The Lamb triumphant looks back upon the sufferings of the Lamb slain. How dear to him are the people whom through his agony he saved, since we love the most tenderly those for whom we suffer most! Now, too, they are throned with him. His conflict and his victory belong to them; their conflict and their victory were in and through him. Associated in the sufferings, they are associated in the exaltation, and together they look upon the symbol of both.

EVERLASTING SECURITY OF THE GLORIFIED.

This, too, is for eternity; for I look upon the symbol as also emblematic of the everlasting security of the redeemed in heaven. Not only are the sins and the sorrows that wellnigh destroyed them on earth left behind, but none like them shall ever enter their blood-bought mansions. After the flood God said to Noah, "I will remember my covenant, which is between me and you, and every living creature of all flesh; and the waters shall no more become a flood to destroy all flesh. And the bow shall be in the cloud; and I will look upon it that I may remember the everlasting covenant between God and every living creature of all flesh that is upon the earth." Gen. ix. 15–17. Every time, then, that Noah and his descendants saw the bow, if they trusted in the promise of God, they knew that the world was safe in the future from any such destruction as had lately passed upon it. How great was the joy of the assurance that it gave!

" When o'er the green, undeluged earth
　　Heaven's covenant it did shine,
　How came the world's gray fathers forth
　　To watch its sacred sign!

" And when its yellow lustre smiled
　　O'er mountains yet untrod,
　Each mother held aloft her child
　　To bless the bow of God."

At first there may have been trembling ones who, when the rain continued for several days at a time, began to fear that another flood might come ; but now all who see the beautiful sign and rest in God's assurance know that every storm, however long continued, shall cease and the world not be drowned by it.

The bow encircling the throne of God also assures us that the redeemed who have reached heaven are for ever delivered from sins and sorrows. Their redemption is for everlasting. The wrath of God has spent its force. The blessed spirits of the just made perfect have no fear of any future wrath. " The Lord shall give thee rest from thy sorrow, and from thy fear, and from the hard bondage wherein thou wast made to serve." Isa. xiii. 3 Sin, with suffering in its train, shall not enter heaven. Within the

4

charmed circle of God's presence it can find no
foothold The glorified are holy and happy for
ever and ever.*   " The inhabitant shall not say,
I am sick ; the people that dwell therein shall be
forgiven their iniquity " Isa xxxiii. 24. "They
shall hunger no more, neither thirst any more;
neither shall the sun light on them, nor any heat.

* It is the manifest teaching of the Bible that the glorified
redeemed are, beyond the possibility of fall, established in holiness and bliss.   But there are some who, while holding that
"they will be so entirely confirmed that they will be for ever free
from all danger of sinning," say that " the *possibility* of sinning
will, however, still remain, as it was with man in his original
innocence, and as it is with the holy angels."—*Knapp* This is
analogous to the scholastic question of the peccability or impec-
cability of Christ's human nature—whether his sinlessness
sprang from a *posse non peccare* or a *non posse peccare.* The
revealed facts are, that he triumphantly resisted temptation, and
that in the future world his redeemed people shall never be
exposed to temptations. Knapp's own comparison is against his
admission; for if our first parents had stood their term of proba-
tion, the race would have been established beyond the possibility of fall; and Jesus has done for his people what Adam failed
to do   Now, therefore, they "shall never perish." They eat of
the tree of life. Rev. ii 7. They shall not be hurt of the second death ii. 11. Their names shall never be blotted out of
the book of life. iii. 5   They shall go no more out of heaven
iii 12. They shall sit with Christ in his throne, even as Christ is
set down with the Father in his throne. iii 21.

For the Lamb which is in the midst of the throne shall feed them, and shall lead them unto living fountains of water: and God shall wipe away all tears from their eyes." Rev. vii. 16, 17. "And there shall be no more death, neither sorrow nor crying, neither shall there be any more pain: for the former things are passed away." Rev. xxi. 4.

> " No sickness there—
> No weary wasting of the frame away,
>   No fearful shrinking from the midnight air,
> No dread of summer's bright and fervid ray.
>
> " No hidden grief,
> No wild and cheerless vision of despair,
>   No vain petition for a sweet relief,
> No tearful eyes, no broken hearts, are there.
>
> " No parted friends
> O'er mournful recollections have to weep;
>   No bed of death enduring love attends
> To watch the coming of a pulseless sleep." *

" In a little wrath I hid my face from thee for a moment; but with everlasting kindness will I have mercy on thee, saith the Lord, thy Redeemer. For this is as the waters of Noah unto

---

* From an exceedingly musical anonymous poem on pp. 250, 251 in *The Book of Poetry*, issued by the Presbyterian Board of Publication.

me: for as I have sworn that the waters of Noah should no more go over the earth, so have I sworn that I would not be wroth with thee nor rebuke thee. For the mountains shall depart, and the hills be removed; but my kindness shall not depart from thee, neither shall the covenant of my peace be removed, saith the Lord that hath mercy on thee. O thou afflicted, tossed with tempest, and not comforted! behold, I will lay thy stones with fair colors, and lay thy foundations with sapphires." Isa. liv. 8–11.

THE NATURE OF THE HEAVENLY REST.

Pervading the descriptions of the everlasting condition of the redeemed is the *rest* which is thus symbolized in the bow as the very atmosphere of the glorious land.

A voice from the place itself commanded the beloved disciple to write: "Blessed are the dead which die in the Lord, from henceforth: yea, saith the Spirit, that they may rest from their labors, and their works do follow them." Rev. xiv. 13.

The great apostle to the Gentiles, encompassed by troubles and addressing troubled fellow-Christians, wrote: "We are bound to thank God always for you, brethren, as it is meet, because that your faith groweth exceedingly, and the charity of every one of you all toward each other aboundeth; so that we ourselves glory in you in the churches of God, for your patience and faith in all your persecutions and tribulations that ye endure; which is a manifest token of the right-eous judgment of God, that ye may be counted worthy of the kingdom of God, for which ye also suffer; seeing it is a righteous thing with God to recompense tribulation to them that trouble you; and to you, who are troubled, *rest with us,* when the Lord Jesus shall be revealed from heaven with his mighty angels, in flaming fire taking vengeance on them that know not God, and that obey not the gospel of our Lord Jesus Christ; who shall be punished with everlasting destruction from the presence of the Lord, and from the glory of his power; when he shall come to be glorified in his saints, and to be admired in all them that believe in that day." 2 Thess. i. 3–10.

But the rest which is thus held up as the crown-ing and all-permeating blessing of heaven is most assuredly not a passive painless condition. All the visions of the better land throb with an inten-ser and more varied activity than marks our life

here—incessant and heightened activity in knowing, worshiping and serving God.   " Now we see
as through a glass darkly; but then face to face;
now I know in part; but then shall I know even
as also I am known." 1 Cor. xiii. 12.   " They rest
not day and night." Rev. iv. 8.   " Therefore, are
they before the throne of God, and serve him day
and night in his temple; and He that sitteth on
the throne shall dwell among them " Rev. vii.
15.   " And there shall be no more curse: but the
throne of God and of the Lamb shall be in it;
and his servants shall serve him: and they shall
see his face; and his name shall be in their fore-
heads " Rev. xxii. 3, 4.

Activity is the very essence of life   " True,
the soul must begin its activities with the awaken-
ing of the senses; but when it is once awakened,
it never sleeps, so far as we can observe or infer.
If the senses should furnish it no new objects, it
might go on without intermitting its action, busy-
ing itself with the materials already furnished, under laws of its own   We grant also that what
it perceives and desires and does is determined,
to a very great extent, by the objects which
present themselves from without; but these
direct the course of its action by furnishing its

objects ; they do not cause it to act. We con-
cede even that its energy in action is dependent
on material conditions, as the tension and health-
ful harmony of the nervous system. When the
nerves are relaxed or disturbed, as in fainting or
disease, the force of the soul is greatly weakened
or frightfully disordered; but there is no proof
that any bodily conditions can arrest psychical
activity after it has once been aroused." *

When the soul passes from the body at death
it escapes from all that weakens and disorders it,
and with a disembodied mode of energy enters
upon the perfectly holy and happy stage of its
persistent life ; and at the resurrection day it shall
be re-embodied in the spiritual form, and therein
act and work on for evermore with all its capacities
and faculties

The intensely metaphysical and devotional Augustine has, at the close of his remarkable *Confessions*, admirably combined these elements of
activity and rest, not as alternating one with the
other, but existing together :

"O Lord God, give peace unto us, the *peace
of rest*, the peace of the Sabbath which hath no
evening For all this most goodly array of

* Porter's *Elements of Intellectual Science*, pp 18, 19.

things very good,* having finished their courses,
is to pass away, for in them there was morning
and evening. But the seventh day hath no
evening nor hath it setting, because thou hast
sanctified it to an everlasting continuance; that
that which thou didst after thy works which were
very good—namely, resting the seventh day
(*although thou madest them in unbroken rest*), we
too may do, thy book announcing beforehand
unto us that we also after our works (very good,
because thou hast given them to us) *shall rest in
thee also, in the Sabbath of eternal life.* For thou
shalt rest in us, as now thou workest in us, and
thy rest shall be through us, as thy works are
through us. But thou, Lord, *ever workest, and
art ever at rest.* . . . Thou, the one, the good
God, didst never cease doing good. And we also
have some good works of thy gift, but not eternal; after them *we trust to rest in thy great hallow-
ing.* But thou, being the good, which needeth
no good, *art ever at rest,* because *thy rest is
thyself.*"

A living Christian poet has also said both
truthfully and smoothly:

---

* He has been giving an interpretation of the creation work
as contained in the first chapter of Genesis.

" Service there is rest,
Rest, service ; for the Paradise of saints,
Like Eden with its toilless husbandry,
Has many plants to tend and flowers to twine,
And fruit trees in the garden of the soul,
That ask the culture of celestial skill."

Included in the cessation of the conflict with sin, and relief from the painful effects of sin, which characterize the bliss of heaven, is this *everlasting exemption from weariness* which is the grand peculiarity of the heavenly rest as consistent with perpetual activity.

As we use the word *labor*, there is involved in it the notion of that which results in exhaustion ; and from this all who enter the better land are for ever freed.

" There the weary be at rest." Job iii. 17.

" The righteous is taken away from the evil. He shall enter into peace   They shall rest in their beds; walking in his uprightness." Isa. lvii. 1, 2.

There will be in heaven the continued, unintermitted exercise of all the powers of our mind, and, after the resurrection, of the spiritual body. We are only happy as we use the powers which God has conferred upon us, and are brought into contact with the objects that satisfy them   And we shall

continue to find these exciting objects in heaven.
The glorified souls will eternally be drinking in
of knowledge, and acting upon it. There shall
evermore be something new for them to perceive.
New views in Nature shall burst upon their enraptured gaze. New revelations of God's providence
and grace shall be opened up to their admiring
contemplation. As they roam at will through
the boundless expanse of the universe, ever near
God's throne, however far from it, one object after
another shall cross their path, and lead them to
cry out anew, " Oh the depth of the riches both
of the wisdom and knowledge of God! How
unsearchable are his judgments, and his ways
past finding out!" The time will never come
when they shall cease to learn of God, or simply
gaze in retrospective meditation upon themselves
or upon the acquisitions of the past, immense as
they may be. Through an eternity of ages, there
shall be unrolled before them God's great books,
leaf after leaf attracting their attention and ministering food for their support. Memory will bring
before them the past. Imagination will have a
grander, freer scope for its majestic exercise.
Still, there shall be room for the exercise of judgment and the drawing out of long chains of

reasoning, for it belongs to God alone to know all truth intuitively. The pure and holy affections shall ever glow at a white heat. Useful works for God, in forms and places which we cannot now conceive, shall engage the sinless capacities and powers that have been developed and trained in this life.

But none of these activities shall be accompanied by the weariness that creeps in upon us here. After the work of the day, bodily toilers, physically prostrated, must lie down and rest. There is a limit in study beyond which the man of the strongest intellect cannot go, however greatly he may be delighted with and excited by his mental efforts. From day to day he must pause for a part of the time, and during some seasons of the year indulge a longer abstinence. Even from our labors as co-workers with God for the salvation of souls there must be cessations, so as to recover from bodily weakness and mental prostration. Periods of exertion resulting in weariness and calling for repose—such is our life here.

That blessed state to which we are looking, however, is an eternal rest, not from exertion itself, but from the exhaustion which follows it here as a part of the curse on sin and as one of the steps to death: "In the sweat of thy face

shalt thou eat bread, till thou return unto the
ground." Gen. iii. 19.   Work shall never be
suspended, but it shall just as certainly never
weaken or wear out.

"This is the rest wherewith ye may cause the
weary to rest.   And this is the refreshing." Isa.
xxviii 12.

In this, Christianity meets the highest demands
of our nature.   There are false religions which
tell their deluded followers of a Paradise of sensual pleasures, in which they shall never be called
upon to make any effort for themselves, but shall
be ministered to by the most beautiful of creatures.   Our religion, coming from the Author of
our existence, strikes deeper into our being, and
assures us that the time is coming to the people
of God when every native power of mind and
body will be unceasingly occupied, but no
exhaustion be produced, no lassitude fallen into.
A mortal frame, pervaded by a nervous system
most delicately organized and as easily played
upon by passing events as is the Æolian harp by
the gentlest breeze, shall not hamper the soul in
the study of God's works and in the doing of his
will—to-day bright, to-morrow dull; to-day soar-
ing grandly through heaven, to-morrow down in

the depths and moaning over its pains and its listlessness; to-day finding a pleasure in communion with God, and to-morrow driven away from him. There shall be none of these aberrations and variations in the sinless land. The perfection of the everlasting rest shall be that its possessors will uniformly, without pain, exercise their powers to their highest enjoyment. The aroma of worship will be about all their employments. God shall be all in all to them, and they shall never tire in their worship and work, nor ever desire to cease from the precious prosecution of them. Alternation in the forms of activity shall be their great means of recreation.

"Hast thou not known? hast thou not heard, that the everlasting God, the Lord, the Creator of the ends of the earth, fainteth not, neither is weary? There is no searching of his understanding. He giveth power to the faint, and to them that have no might he increaseth strength. Even the youths shall faint and be weary, and the young men shall utterly fall; but they that wait upon the Lord shall renew their strength; they shall mount up with wings as eagles; they shall run, and not be weary; and they shall walk, and not faint." Isa. xl. 28–31.

Hence the apostle designates the whole future state of bliss as a Sabbath into which the redeemed enter: "There remaineth, therefore a rest—*a keeping of the Sabbath*—to the people of God." Heb. iv. 9—"a home for the exile, a mansion for the pilgrim, a Sabbath for the workman weary of the world's week-day toil. In time there are many Sabbaths, but then there shall be one, perfect and eternal." *

A perfect Sabbath here would be a day in which nothing sinful should distract our attention, but the whole time should be spent in the work of God and in communion with him and with each other, and whose spiritual and joyous activities should be accompanied by no weariness. But such a perfect season comes to none of us here.

* The different words translated *rest* in our version of the Bible are suggestive of the fullness of the heavenly bliss. In Heb. iv. 8 it is "*catapausis*—Hebrew *noah*—rest from weariness, as the ark rested on Ararat after its tossings; as Israel under Joshua rested from war in Canaan. *Anesis* (2 Thess. i. 7), *relaxation* from afflictions *Anapausis*, 'rest' given by Jesus now (Matt. xi. 28); but the 'rest' (Heb. iv. 9) is the nobler (Hebrew) '*Sabbath*' *rest*—literally, cessation from work finished (v. 5.), as God rested. Rev. xiv. 13; xvi. 17. The two ideas combined give the perfect view of the heavenly Sabbath—rest from weariness sorrow and sin, and rest in the completion of God's new creation. Rev xxi 5."

It remains, however, for the people of God. It *remains !* It is in the future, but it is certain and will be unending. Up there! Beyond the dark river! In the exceeding brightness of God's own presence! At the end of earth's ascending and toilsome journey! And it "shall be glorious"! Isa. xi 10.

"Go thy way, till the end be; for thou shalt rest, and stand in thy lot at the end of the days." Dan. xii. 13.

GOD'S SAVING WORK.

3 The bow around the throne is a symbol of the saving work by which the heaven of rest and of glory was secured to sinners, and by which the redeemed are led to it through the sufferings of this life.

REDEMPTION IS OF GRACE.

In sight the rainbow was like unto an emerald. An emerald is green. Green is the central color of this beautiful object of Nature. It is the color on which the eye of man can gaze with the greatest delight. When it has become tired and weak with the blazing reflection of the city pavement, the eye rests upon the greenness of the country fields with the calm repose of satisfaction. The

rainbow is the sign of God's covenant of salvation. Grace is not only the central but the prevalent color of that covenant, for grace and truth
came by Jesus Christ; and that is what the
burdened, heavy-laden, weary sinner looks for.
Nothing but grace, love to the undeserving, can
satisfy him. Redemption is all of grace. All
the other attributes of God are blended in it;
and in heaven the cry of the redeemed, as they
gaze toward the throne of God, will ever be,
"Not unto us, not unto us, but unto thy name
give glory for thy mercy, and for thy truth's
sake." Ps. cxv 1.

"God hath saved us, and called us with an
holy calling, not according to our works, but
according to his own purpose and grace, which
was given us in Christ Jesus before the world
began; but is now made manifest by the appearing of our Saviour Jesus Christ, who hath abolish-
ed death, and hath brought life and immortality
to light through the gospel." 2 Tim. i. 9 There
is the full gospel of redemption as it appears to
the saved from the heights of heaven.

"Being justified freely by his grace through
the redemption that is in Christ Jesus." Rom.
iii 24. "Where sin abounded, grace did much

more abound; that as sin hath reigned unto
death, even so might grace reign through righteousness unto eternal life by Jesus Christ our
Lord." Rom. v. 21, 22. "Blessed be the God
and Father of our Lord Jesus Christ, who hath
blessed us with all spiritual blessings in heavenly
places in Christ: according as he hath chosen us
in him before the foundation of the world, that
we should be holy and without blame before him
in love; having predestinated us unto the adoption of children, according to the good pleasure
of his will, to the praise of the glory of his grace,
wherein he hath made us accepted in the Beloved." Eph. i. 3–6. "God, who is rich in mercy,
for his great love wherewith he loved us, even
when we were dead in sins, hath quickened us
together with Christ, and hath raised us up together, and made us sit together in heavenly
places in Christ Jesus: that in the ages to come
he might show the exceeding riches of his grace
in his kindness toward us through Christ Jesus."
Eph. ii. 5–7. "After that the kindness and love
of God our Saviour toward man appeared; not by
works of righteousness which we have done, but
according to his mercy he saved us, by the wash-
ing of regeneration, and renewing of the Holy

5

Ghost; which he shed on us abundantly through
Jesus Christ our Saviour; that being justified by
his grace, we should be made heirs according to
the hope of eternal life." Tit. iii. 4–7.

There is a gushing richness in the words which
the great apostle thus employed, when he was on
earth, to picture his enrapturing redemption.
How he loved to emphasize the word *grace!*
How eager he was to repeat the names of his
Redeemer! How sweeping the mode in which he
carries every blessing back to the eternal fountain
of unmerited love! But with how much more
ecstasy must he now, in the entirely unmarred
and glorious enjoyment of his salvation, repeat the
words which he was once inspired to write! How
seraphic his worship as with them he bursts into
the grateful song of eternity! And to all of the
glorified, as they look upon the bow-encircled
throne, the terms express their full import while
in the rapture of triumph they evermore repeat
them.

BUT MANIFESTS HOLINESS AND JUSTICE.

But the rainbow encircles the throne of God,
who is compared to a jasper and a sardine stone.
These represent him as the holy and the just

One. While grace is the prevailing aspect of the bow of promise, it appears upon the deep background of the divine holiness and justice, which are unsullied in their purity and unbroken in their requirements ; for in the gospel of salvation the grace of God comes to us through Jesus Christ, and Jesus in his death suffered for sinners, enduring in their place the dread penalty of the immutable law and satisfying for them the extremest demands of divine justice. Now, therefore, God, though surprisingly gracious, is strictly just while he justifies sinners (Rom. iii. 26), because Christ in his life and his death is the end of the law for righteousness. Rom. x. 4. He "hath redeemed us from the curse of the law, being made a curse for us." Gal. iii. 13. "He gave himself for our sins, that he might deliver us from this present evil world, according to the will of God and our Father; to whom be the glory for ever and ever." Gal. i. 4, 5.*

* Dr. Shedd makes a remark about the experience of Augustine which pithily expresses the relation of the divine attributes in our salvation : " He does not presume to cast himself upon the divine mercy until he has first recognized and acquiesced in the divine justice." In this he illustrated the most scriptural type of conversion.

THE HOLINESS OF THE REDEEMED.

Furthermore, the Redeemer, through the Holy
Spirit, makes all his redeemed holy, so that when
they enter heaven the unspotted purity of the
place is not outraged by their presence. " Without
holiness no man shall see the Lord." Heb. xii. 14.
This truth is as unbending as it was before the
Fall. But Christ by his Spirit purifies all his
people, and takes them to be with him for ever.
" The grace of God, that bringeth salvation, hath
appeared to all men, teaching us that, denying
ungodliness and worldly lusts, we should live
soberly, righteously, and godly in this present
world; looking for that blessed hope and the
glorious appearing of our great God and Saviour
Jesus Christ; who gave himself for us that he
might redeem us from all iniquity, and purify
unto himself a peculiar people, zealous of good
works." Tit. ii. 11–15. Hence in heaven, around
the throne of God, grace rejoices not against
justice, nor justice against grace, nor does holiness suffer from either; but as the variously-
colored rainbow is composed of three primary
colors, so these attributes of God are firmly
connected side by side, forming the centre of
heaven's arch—grace resting upon justice, and

holiness rising out of grace—and enveloping in their beautiful halo all the other divine attributes. For they all are operative in redemption. To the popular view there are seven colors in the bow. Nothing is more beautiful than the gradation and intermingling of them. So with the perfections of the Deity in the work of salvation through Jesus Christ. " God is a Spirit, infinite, eternal and unchangeable, in his being, wisdom, power, holiness, justice, goodness and truth." Thus he appears, with all his attributes, in salvation. Not one of them is wanting. Not one has failed to fulfill its part. All are beautifully symbolized in this vision. And the glorified see God as he is, because they are perfect like him.

THREEFOLD ENERGY OF REDEMPTION.

Again: the light of the sun, which shines through the raindrops and is reflected in the prismatic colors of the rainbow, has three energies—light, heat and chemical power. Not only do the light and the heat which bless the earth stream down from the great luminary, but science tell us that all the force that is stored up in the world was drawn from it. We can also trace the power of the Redeemer in the application of redemption to the individual soul, as energizing itself in a threefold manner.

The unconverted soul is asleep in the darkness of ignorance; in regeneration the light of Christ shines around it, and his voice is heard: "Awake, thou that sleepest, and arise from the dead, and Christ shall give thee light." Eph. v. 14.

The spiritually dead soul is cold, as certainly as the dead body is; the grace of Christ revives and warms it, and sets it all aglow with love to him. The Spirit lights the fire of pure affections, which burn up in an unquenchable flame toward heaven, and diffuse a warmth that is preparative for the glorious life.

There is further a mighty expulsive and impulsive force in the grace of Christ. It casts sin from the heart, and it sends the saved soul forth in a life of holiness and active effort for the glory of God. If we walk in the light, as he is in the light, the blood of Jesus Christ cleanseth us from all sin. I John i. 7.

Light, heat, energetic activity—these are involved in salvation. None of us are saved without them. The rainbow of heaven may remind us of the way in which the Spirit brought us first to grace, and then to glory.

THE TRIUNE GOD.

The threefold personality of the Godhead also is exhibited in redemption. God is revealed as the Father, the Son, and the Holy Spirit—the Father devising, the Son procuring, the Holy Spirit applying, salvation. Neither can be degraded from the equal glory of the others. They are all represented in the vision of which the rainbow is a prominent feature. God the Father is first upon the throne. Seven lamps of fire, which are the seven spirits of God, are before the throne. Seven is in prophecy the symbol of perfection, and here this emblem represents the perfect Spirit of God, with the varied and complete graces with which he replenishes his Church. The crucified Lamb of God is also seen and worshiped as well as the Father. The glory of the triune God in the work of salvation is thus reflected from the dark clouds of sin.

MANIFESTATION OF THE DIVINE GLORY.

In redemption the divine glory is brightly manifested. The rainbow is beautiful, but without a storm, without a passing cloud, without descending raindrops, it does not appear. It comes after darkness and gloom, and the contrast

makes its light the more charming and attractive.
So the salvation of sinners brings greater glory
to God than creation did. Satan introduced sin
to mar the work of God's hand; God overrules
the designs of the evil one, and reveals his own
perfections in the most striking manner to the
universe.   The Church makes known unto principalities and powers in heavenly places the manifold wisdom of God, according to the eternal
purpose which he purposed in Christ Jesus our
Lord. Eph. iii. 10. There is a grandeur in redemption which creation, beautiful as it was, had
not. God in Christ turns darkness into light,
overcomes sin with holiness, and takes men, who
were made lower than the angels, into a position
far above them all. The incarnation of the Son
of God, his death upon the cross, and his ascension to the throne of the universe,—these truths
are written upon the bow of promise, and throughout eternity attract the admiration of redeemed
men and of the unfallen angels. It is no marvel
that the whole creation is represented as joining
with the redeemed in the admiring worship:
" Blessing and honor and glory and power be
unto Him that sitteth upon the throne, and
unto the Lamb, for ever and ever!" Rev. v. 13.

These are some of the lessons which, in the interpretation of Scripture with a sober use of the imagination and without being fanciful, we may draw from this part of the visions of the Apocalypse. They are very delightful and very alluring. Let me bind them together in one paragraph, and give them to the children of God as precious subjects for meditation.

The judgments which are denounced in the Bible against a world of sinners shall not harm you; the everlasting God is pledged for your safety. You are passing, it is true, through a world in which storms of sorrow perpetually arise. But before you is the place of rest from them all, in which the remembrance of the salvation that came to you and delivered you from them shall far outweigh your temporary troubles. Yea, even the storms of earth are sanctifying. The divine love pervades them. With peculiar tenderness Jesus shall evermore remember his life of sorrows. That now binds him very intimately to the children of affliction; and through eternity you shall with him enjoy the happiness which has gushed forth from the fountain of his sufferings. The justice and the love of God are united in securing your pardon for the past, and by holiness fitting you for the unending future. Your eternal safety is therefore involved in the glory of the redeeming Godhead. Whenever you see the rainbow in the clouds let it remind you of these most comforting truths;

> " For, faithful to its sacred page,
>   Heaven still rebuilds its span,
>   Nor lets the type grow pale with age
>   That first spoke peace to man."

II.

THE GREAT CITY: THE NUMBER OF THE
REDEEMED.

IN the visions of the apocalyptic seer the twenty-first chapter of the book of Revelation follows the resurrection and the general judgment. Prophetically, the judgment day has come and gone; the wicked, with Satan as their great leader, have been cast into the lake of fire ; the conflagration of the last day has regenerated and renovated the world of matter ; and the new heavens and the new earth have emerged from the baptismal fire, when John is taken away by an angel to a high mountain, whence he sees a great city pendent in the air before him.

As becomes the peroration of such a magnificent and varied discourse as the Divine Volume really is, this is perhaps the richest of all the heavenly visions. It encloses the most comfort-

ing truths, and is garnished with the most musical
expressions. Gems of brilliant and enrapturing
beauty are encased in it.

THE NEW JERUSALEM.

In describing his vision the apostle first designates the new Jerusalem, which he thus beholds
as "a bride adorned for her husband." V. 2. By
this term Christ's redeemed people, in their col-
lective capacity, are characterized in the Bible;
for "the husband is the head of the wife, even as
Christ is the Head of the Church; and he is the
Saviour of the body. . . . Husbands, love your
wives, even as Christ also loved the Church and
gave himself for it." Eph. v. 23–25. Then the
seer proceeds to describe them literally as a
city.   First he beholds the people; then the
place in which through eternity they shall dwell;
and he applies to both the same name.

THE CITY AND THE PEOPLE.

The question has, therefore, been keenly controverted whether the new Jerusalem is actually
the abode of the heavenly citizens, or only a representation of the Church triumphant under the
emblem of a city. I suppose the true view to be
that it "is both real and typical, an actual city,

of which every part typifies the spiritual temple of living stones. For as the glorified body will be the worthy habitation of the perfectly sancti-fied spirit, so the celestial city will be the meet dwelling-place of the saints for ever, and their spiritual characteristics will each and all find a counterpart in that marvelous structure prepared for them by their God." The everlasting dwell-ing-place of Christ's redeemed Church, after the resurrection, appears on the panorama of prophecy. The name and the images that are employed are applicable to the people and to their city; and the wondrous mutual relation of the two causes the description to pass rapidly, and almost indistin-guishably perhaps, from one to the other. " For, in the first place, it is most common in all lan-guages to denote by the same term, as London, sometimes the city, sometimes the mass of its in-habitants, and sometimes the complex of the two. This was common amongst the writers of the Scriptures The scriptural uses of Zion, Babylon, Tyre will present themselves as illustrations to the minds of all. And, secondly, a material city is frequently a type of its inhabitants or of the state of which it is the capital. No one can visit Rome without being impressed with the fact that, in its combined ruin and grandeur, its death and life, the existing city is itself the type of the existing Roman Church. This in old times was true of Babylon, of Athens, of Tyre, of Rome, and especially of Jerusalem. And doubtless it is in great measure owing to this fact that a city and its inhabitants are so generally designated by one and the same name. In the judgment of the writer, as the old Jerusalem symbolized the Israel of which it was the capital, so the new Jerusalem will symbolize the glorified community of whom it will be the abode and capital." *

Passing by the other features of the description, which will in other connections and forms appear through subsequent portions of the book, I shall here concentrate the attention on the expressions that reveal the size of heaven and the number of its redeemed inhabitants.

"THAT GREAT CITY."

The place is "that great city."† V. 10. It "lieth four-square, and the length is as large as the

---

* Dr. E. R. Craven in *Lange on the Revelation*, p. 390.

† Textual criticism, based on examination of different ancient versions, rejects the adjective. I retain it here as a familiar English expression, which contains and condenses the truth as taught in other undoubted passages.

breadth; and he measured the city with the reed, twelve thousands furlongs. And the length and the breadth and the height of it are equal." V. 16. A cubed city, fifteen hundred miles long and broad and high! "And the *nations* of them which are saved shall walk in the light of it." *

Curious calculations have been made as to the capacity of a city which is so large, and as to the number of inhabitants which it would contain. They are, however, more curious than useful. They give the mind no definite idea.† The

* The best texts read, "And the nations shall walk by means of her light."

† Here is one: "Twelve thousand furlongs—7,920,000 feet—which, being cubed, is 948,988,000,000,000,000,000,000 cubic feet, the half of which we will reserve for the throne of God and the court of heaven, half of the balance for the streets; and the remainder, divided by 496, the cubical feet in the rooms 19 feet square and 16 feet high, will be 5,743,759,000,000 rooms. We will now suppose the world always did and always will contain 900,000,000 inhabitants, and a generation will last $33\frac{1}{3}$ years (2,700,000,000 every century), and that the world stands 100,000 years = 27,000,000,000,000 persons. Then suppose there were 11,230 such worlds, equal to this number of inhabitants and duration of years; then there would be a room 16 feet long and 17 feet wide and 15 feet high for each person; and yet there would be room." Even if the reservations and the suppositions of such a calculation had a real basis, and the arithmetic

great truth which is pictured by the seer is exhibited in grand and literal terms in other passages of the word of God

The completed Church of the redeemed, after the resurrection and the judgment, embracing the departed of all ages from Abel down to the last saint who shall fall asleep in Jesus, and those who shall be still living at the second coming of the Lord, is in prophetic vision settling in its everlasting abode. What does the pen of inspiration elsewhere teach us as to the number, the character, the relation of those who shall compose the holy and happy society?*

Let the question be answered, and the vision be soberly yet exultingly read, in the light of

were correct, the impression of absurdity which these huge figures make upon our minds illustrates the superior wisdom which marks God's mode of revealing heaven to us

* I intentionally abstain from discussing or dwelling at any length upon disputed questions as to the chronological relation of this vision and the place of the redeemed in their resurrection state. What I have said will indicate the views which I hold, but I have desired here to give them as little prominence as possible, and to say only what is necessary to introduce the subjects of the book. My objects are practical, and the great themes which I shall treat do not depend on any particular interpretation of the points referred to, but will be accepted by those who differ on them.

other explicit teachings of the holy oracles. To the law and to the testimony. Very rich and grace-magnifying are their declarations on this point.

THE REDEEMED INCALCULABLY NUMEROUS.

1. The number of the inhabitants of heaven will be incalculably great.*

This promise was made to Abraham: "I will multiply thy seed as the stars of heaven, and as the sand which is upon the seashore." Gen. xxii. 17. Again: "I will make thy seed as the dust of the earth, so that if a man can number the dust of the earth, then shall thy seed also be numbered." Gen. xiii. 16. Yet again to Jacob: "Thy seed shall be as the dust of the earth, and thou shalt spread abroad to the west and to the east, and to the north and to the south, and in thee and in thy seed shall all the families of the

---

* Romanism seems to minify rather than magnify on this point. Thus Massillon in his celebrated sermon on " The Small Number of the Saved:" " There are only these two ways of salvation; heaven is only open to the innocent or to the penitent. . . . To die innocent is a grace to which few souls can aspire, and to live penitent is a mercy which the relaxed state of our morals renders equally rare." *All* the unbaptized, even infants, are by this system excluded from heaven.

6

earth be blessed " Gen. xxviii. 14. In the same
line the Lord declared through the prophet,
"As the host of heaven cannot be numbered,
neither the sand of the sea measured, so will I
multiply the seed of David my servant, and the
Levites that minister unto me." Jer. xxxiii. 22.

These promises did not receive their fulfillment
in the multiplication of the natural descendants
of Abraham; for, says the inspired apostle Paul,
addressing Gentile believers, in Gal. iii. 29,
"If ye be Christ's, then are ye Abraham's seed,
and heirs according to the promise."

The saved of the human race, then, form an
innumerable host.

When we gaze with the naked eye upon the
heavens, on a beautifully clear evening, we might
think that with a little patience we could number
the stars; but as telescope after telescope of increased power sweeps the vast concave of blue
they appear like "dust scattered through the
immensity of space." Worlds upon worlds, suns
upon suns, systems upon systems, multiply before
the piercing eye of the astronomer. As far as
the mightiest glass can reach, the universe is
peopled with them. The light of multitudes
which had not touched the earth when Abraham

lived now impinge upon us. " The host of heaven
cannot be numbered " by man The assertion is
not a poetical one It is not a flight of fancy.
It is sober fact.* Neither have the sands of

* The fixed stars have been divided by astronomers into six-
teen classes, according to their different degrees of brightness
Six of those classes are visible to our naked eye, the othe ten
only through telescopes. And here are the numbers of them :
In the first magnitude, 20, in the second, 60; in the third, 190;
in the fourth, 425, in the fifth, 1100; in the sixth, 4000.
These are all that the naked eye can see. But those visible
through telescopes are—in the seventh, 26,000; the eighth,
180,000; the ninth, 1,100,000, the tenth, 7,000,000; the
eleventh, 50,000,000; the twelfth, 300,000,000; the thirteenth,
500,000,000; while the other three classes are literally innumerable Each of these stars is probably a sun larger than ours,
and the centre of a planetary system similar to ours. Theie
have been discovered nearly 6000 nebulous firmaments, each
composed of innumerable suns and systems. Our Milky Way is
one of them, and it alone is estimated to contain 18,000,000
or 20,000,000 suns, it consisting, as Herschel says, " of stars
scattered by millions like glittering dust on the black ground of
the general heavens " There was infinitely more than Abraham
could understand, more than with our wonderful astronomical
progress we can fathom, in God's promise that the spiritual descendants of the patriarch should be as " the stars of the
heavens." But wonderful as they thus are, " He telleth the
number of the stars; he calleth them *all* by their names." Ps.
cxlvii. 4 And so he knows each of us; nay, not even a sparrow falleth to the ground without him.

the seashore, nor the particles of the dust of the earth, been computed.

God has never, since the Fall, been without a seed to serve him. From the time of Abel down to this hour the narrow path from earth to heaven has never been destitute of travelers. Through the pearly gates of the beautiful city an immense host have already entered upon the enjoyment of the eternal rest. Still the saved are pressing on. From land to land, from age to age, down to the hour of the judgment, pilgrims shall continue to add to the number of the glorified. The redemption of human beings was precious. The Son of God came from heaven to earth to save them. He sent not an angel. He sent not hosts of angels. He came himself. He gave himself, his life, his precious blood, a ransom for lost sinners of mankind. His mission was extraordinary. The value of the atonement which he made is beyond the computation of all the rules of arithmetic. Neither human nor angelic power can estimate it. The multitude who receive its benefits, and enter the celestial mansions as trophies of the Redeemer's wonderful grace, will also exceed the grasp of finite calculation.

It has been the fanciful idea of some that the

number of saved men will repair the loss which heaven experienced in the banishment from it of the apostate angels. "So many angels as fell from heaven, so many souls shall ascend to heaven," says one our American poets.* We cannot stop with that limit. Redemption is more glorious than creation. Man restored will occupy a higher position than did man unfallen. The regenerate earth will be more beautiful than was the world on which Adam was placed. On the same principle we may feel assured that the number of the saved will more than make up for the loss of the rebellious angels, who, after their fall, tried to carry the whole human race with them. When at the last day our Lord Jesus Christ presents to the Father his blood-bought Church, complete and glorious, not having spot or wrinkle, or any such thing, saying, "Here am I and those whom thou hast given me," he will fill heaven with an inconceivable number of inhabitants; for, cries out the inspired seer in ecstasy, "I beheld, and lo! a great multitude, which no man could number, of all nations and kindreds, and people, and tongues, stood before the throne and before the Lamb, clothed with white robes and palms in

* Longfellow.

their hands, and cried with a loud voice, saying, Salvation unto our God which sitteth upon the throne, and unto the Lamb!" Rev. vii. 9, 10.

THE IMMENSE MAJORITY OF THE HUMAN RACE.

2. The inhabitants of heaven shall not only be an incalculably great multitude, but they will include the immensely larger proportion of the human race.

INFANTS.

Our view on this point must largely be settled by the position that we take in reference to infants. As the greater portion of the human beings who are born into the world die in the dawn of their existence, if the Redeemer takes them to himself they, with believing adults, enroll among the saved from age to age the vast majority of the descendants of Adam.

(1.) The Bible, which is our only guide in this as in every other question connected with salvation, magnifies the sufficiency of Christ's atoning work. The value of that atonement is infinite. It is abundantly sufficient to save the whole human race. Its definite and personal design lies in the divine purpose alone. We have, therefore, no right to limit its application to any narrower range than that which is expressly indicated by God himself. Our rule should be not to exclude all whom the Bible does not expressly declare to be included, but to include all in the design of Christ's death who are not in express terms declared to be for ever shut out of the kingdom The immoral in life, the unholy in heart, the unloving, the worldly, the disobedient, those who show to the day of their death that they have not been regenerated, are banished from heaven The Bible is addressed to actively intelligent beings, and it tells them that if they do not with the heart believe in the Redeemer, and confess him and repent of sin, they cannot be saved. But "the Scriptures nowhere exclude any class of infants, baptized or unbaptized, born in Christian or in heathen lands, of believing or unbelieving parents, from the benefits of the redemption of Christ." They teach that, though infants are born under the curse of sin, they can be regenerated. They mention some actual cases of infant regeneration; and, as not the slightest hint is given of infant perdition, those actualities raise the strongest of rational hopes that the salvation of all infants is possible, probable, certain.

(2) The Bible teaches "that it is more conge-
nial with the nature of God to bless than to curse,
to save than to destroy." It was the more spontaneous prompting of his nature to provide salvation than to permit men to fall. Before sin
came, his love made the covenant of redemption.
The parable of the Prodigal Son represents him
as looking for the sinner's return and as going
forth to meet him. Yea, it is his Spirit that has
come to every penitent, and first breathed the
breath of life into the dead soul and caused it to
desire to return to God. Let us never think of
him as a vindictive persecutor who delights in
handing the victims of sin over to the eternal
prison-house. He punishes, but only because
the relation of his unalterably holy nature to sin
makes it imperative. Now, our nature is a tran-
script of his Especially may the yearnings of
regenerate hearts be looked upon as the inspira-
tions of the Holy Ghost, unless they are condemned on the pages of the divine word What
Christian heart, especially in the hour of bereavement, does not indulge the hope and belief, even
though it be with trembling, that the little one is
safe? But let it not be with trembling. David's
conviction that his child had gone home to God

is not condemned by inspiration. It is the conviction of the universal Christian heart; and here
emphatically *vox populi Dei, vox Dei*—the voice
of the people of God is the voice of God. The
iniquities of fathers are no more visited upon
children in the eternal world than human beings
are condemned to eternal death on account of
Adam's sin, and irrespective of their own moral
conduct. Judgment is God's strange work, never
unnecessarily resorted to. How could any one
think that, while the condemned thief, after a life
of infamy, was taken through a penitent faith
from the jaws of death to heaven, young souls
that had not committed the first actual transgression, breathing themselves away from their little
bodies in their mothers' arms, anywhere on the
face of the globe, in the same hour with the terrible crucifixion, were kept out of the door of
eternal bliss?

(3.) The awards of the judgment day are to
be "to every man according to his deeds." Rom.
ii. 6. Stronger still, every one is "to receive the
things done in his body, according to that he hath
done, whether it be good or bad." 2 Cor. v. 10
Not *for* the things, but the things themselves.
Those who die in infancy will have no evil things

to receive back. No such burning treasures of woe are laid up for them. Whether so designed or not, there is no class to whom the description of Rev. xiv. 4, 5 will more unreservedly apply than to infants.*

(4.) One of the Saviour's acts, while in the flesh on earth, seems to have been designed to be symbolical of this precious truth; and the encouraging and rebuking words with which he accompanied it put it in the most authoritative form. "The conduct and language of our Lord in reference to children are not to be regarded as matters of sentiment, or simply expressive of kindly'feeling. He evidently looked upon them as the lambs of the flock for which, as the good Shepherd, he laid down his life, and of whom he said they shall never perish, and no man could pluck them out of his hands. Of such, he tells us, is the kingdom of heaven, as though heaven was, in great measure, composed of the souls of the redeemed infants." Mark x. 13–16 †

* One of the beautiful hymns in Keble's *Christian Year* is suggested by this—" The Holy Innocents "

† Speaking of this incident, Farrar (*Life of Christ*, ii 158) calls attention to the indebtedness of women and children to Christianity. " Women were not honored nor children loved in antiquity as now they are; no halo of romance and tenderness

(5.) And for this reason God has always in-cluded children with their parents in the Church. Infant membership in the Church is based on infant salvation. The presumption is that every child born within it is embraced in the covenant of redemption. Nothing destroys that presumption but a life of transgression, commenced with moral agency and persisted in until death. Those who

encircled them, too often they were subjected to shameful cruel-ties and hard neglect. But He who came to be the friend of all sinners and the helper of all the suffering and the sick, came also to elevate woman to her due honor centuries before the Teutonic element of modern society was dreamt of, and to be the protector and friend of helpless infancy and innocent child-hood." He adds in a note that "the Essenian celibacy rose distinctly out of contempt for and distrust of woman," and that " the author of the apocryphal Ecclesiasticus speaks in the harsh-est tone of women." It is worth while to connect with this the fact to which Charles Kingsley (*Letters and Memoirs*, 299, Am. ed.) calls attention, with an explanation which may not be re-ceived—that Romanism has not in this worked in harmony with Christ: " What has produced more of nobleness, more of prac-tical good, in the human race, than the chivalrous idea of wed-lock which our Teutonic race holds, and which the Romance or popish races of Europe have never to this day grasped with any firm hold?" If the papacy, by its exaltation of Mary, dig-nifies the sex, the practical influence of its idea of the peculiar holiness of celibacy offsets that and pours contempt on women and children.

die in infancy go away from earth surrounded by
the glorious halo of the covenant.   On their
being brought into the world they have a right
to the baptism which signs them with the name
of their Redeemer, which leaves their names
enrolled among his people if they are called in
infancy to his glorious presence, and which binds
them to obedience to him if they are spared on
the earth to adult years.   This does not, as
Romanists do, hand the unbaptized children over
to perdition.*   It raises a belief in the salvation
of all infants, but gives Christian parents the
pledge of it, in the presence of the Church of
God, for theirs.   It is a sign of that regenerating
grace without which no human being can be
saved   Ordinarily, that grace comes in the effec-

* The strict papal doctrine is that the unbaptized cannot be
saved, and therefore that infants dying without baptism are not
at death, or ever after it, admitted into heaven.   Romish coun-
cils have declared that such infants go immediately to hell; but
some of their writers remind us that there are many departments
in hell; and they say that infants in their department suffer
neither sorrow nor sadness in consequence of their deprivation
of the happiness of the saints!   The simple loss of the beatific
vision, not the pain of eternal fire, is the distinction that is thus
sought to be made.   But this is a weak effort to break the force
of the established dogma; for how long are the infants to continue in that puerile condition?

tual call "by his word and Spirit" which enables the adult to embrace the Saviour by faith. The call of the word infants hear not. Faith they cannot exercise. The Spirit can, nevertheless, regenerate them; and their regeneration, as that of adults, is due to God's electing grace. Therefore, says the Westminster Confession, "Elect infants, dying in infancy, are regenerated and saved by Christ, through the Spirit, who worketh when and where and how he pleaseth."

CHILDREN IN HEAVEN.

It will not be out of place to turn aside from the main line of our subject and consider briefly a question which is often raised, especially by bereaved parents: Do those who in infancy are translated to paradise continue children?

The ideas which different persons entertain on this point are shaped by their wishes and peculiar feelings. One view has been presented by Longfellow in his poem "Resignation:"

> "Not as a child shall we again behold her;
> For when with raptures wild
> In our embraces we again enfold her,
> She will not be a child,
>
> "But a fair maiden in her Father's mansion,
> Clothed with celestial grace;

> And beautiful with all the soul's expansion,
>   Shall we behold her face."

Another of the popular writers of the day describes parents who lost in early childhood one of their twin daughters, and " who always pictured to themselves, year after year, the dead child growing in the world beyond the grave, in equal progress, as the living child grew on earth."

" Pet and her baby sister were so exactly alike, and so completely one, that in our thoughts we have never been able to separate them since. It would be of no use to tell us that our dead child was a mere infant. We have changed that child according to the changes in the child spared to us and always with us. As Pet has grown, that child has grown; as Pet has become more sensible and womanly, her sister has become more sensible and womanly by just the same degrees. It would be as hard to convince me that if I was to pass into the other world to-morrow I should not, through the mercy of God, be received there by a daughter just like Pet, as to persuade me that Pet herself is not a reality at my side." *

On the other hand, one of the most religious of poets, in a poem which is of surpassing beauty

* Dickens's *Little Dorrit*, ch. 11.

and grandeur and of Scripture truth in its great
features, though erroneous in some of its drapery,
thus philosophizes on the death of two of his
children :

" A babe in glory is a babe for ever.
  Perfect as spirits, and able to pour forth
  Their glad heart in the tongues which angels use,
  These nurslings gathered in God's nursery
  For ever grow in loveliness and love
  (Growth is the law of all intelligence),
  Yet cannot pass the limit which defines
  Their being. They have never fought the fight,
  Nor borne the heat and burden of the day,
  Nor staggered underneath the weary cross ;
  Conceived in sin, they sinned not ; though they died,
  They never shuddered with the fear of death :
  These things they know not, and can never know.
  Yet, fallen children of a fallen race,
  And early to transgression, like the rest,
  Sure victims, they were bought with Jesus' blood,
  And cleansed by Jesus' Spirit, and redeemed
  By his omnipotent arm from death and hell :
  A link betwixt mankind and angelhood :
  As born of woman, sharers with all saints
  In that great ransom paid upon the cross ;
  In purity and inexperience
  Of guilt akin to angels. Infancy
  Is one thing, manhood one." *

* Bickersteth's *Yesterday, To-Day and For Ever.*

Leigh Hunt also writes: "Those who have lost an infant are never, as it were, without an infant child. Their other children grow up to manhood and womanhood, and suffer all the changes of mortality, but this one alone is rendered an immortal child; for death has arrested it with his kindly harshness, and blessed it into an eternal image of youth and innocence."

These two views differ more in appearance and in their superficial expression than in reality. At the root they agree.

Some who ask the question that has been raised, think of the physical appearance of a child, and their inquiry amounts to this: Does the body of a departed infant grow up into the body of an adult?

But it must be observed that this question cannot apply to the present condition of glorified children, for they wear no body now, and shall not wear any until the resurrection. Between death and the resurrection the soul is disembodied in its heavenly mansion. Then, as to the body after the resurrection, we know nothing about its appearance or size. The Bible teaches expressly that the raised spiritual body shall be the same as the present natural body, but in its outward appearance it shall be, in many respects, very different from it.

As to the infant-soul that is taken to heaven, I conceive these principles to be credible : It enters the Father's house just as it leaves this lower world, though perfectly pure, and free from all those tendencies to sin which here break forth as children reach the age of moral agency. It takes with it none of the experiences of adult life, none of its recollections, none of its formed habits, none of its treasures. It passes into its celestial mansion a babe. Infant-souls in heaven ? Yes. But the child learns. It is taught by Jesus. It learns from those who have gone before it, and who have acquired the rich treasures of experience. As it grows in acquisitions of knowledge and in activity, it also increases its notes of praise to God.

In recollections of earth's life it will always be a babe, for it cannot remember conflicts with temptations which were never had, nor strifes with heart-sins which were never waged, nor sanctified trials which were never endured, nor labors for Jesus which were never performed. In many respects its heavenly life will always be different from that of the veteran in the cause

7

of the Redeemer who laid off his armor after the combats of years.

But in intelligence it certainly shall not continue to be an infant.

You lost a child a few years ago. That child is wiser now than you; and when you go to it you shall find that in many things you will be a learner from it.

It oftentimes happens that, by a wonderful intuitive power, children can strike off sparks of light which give new ideas to their parents. Doubtless in heaven that exists in a higher degree.

This, however, is one of the aspects of our immortality which, perhaps in condescension to the weakness of human thought and wish, God has left to be filled in.

It is "hard for us to say exactly how and in what form we hope to meet again the dear ones who have gone before us." It may be natural to think of the little one as it left you. Perhaps, in the case of the greater number, "the brother or sister or child that died long ago remains in remembrance the same young thing for ever. Many years are past, and we have grown older and more careworn since our last sister died, but *she* never grows older with the passing years; and if God spares us to fourscore we never shall think of her as other than the youthful creature she faded." *

But it may be that the explanation of this is found in the words of a thoughtful writer:

"A fond mother loses her infant. What more tender than the hope she has to meet it again in heaven? Does she really, then, expect to find a little child in heaven?—some angel nursling that she may eternally take to her bosom, fondle and caress? Oh, do not ask her. I would not have her ask herself. The consolatory vision springs spontaneously from the mother's grief. It is Nature's own remedy. She gave that surpassing love, and a grief as poignant must follow. She cannot take away that grief; she half transforms it to a hope." †

A RICH MANIFESTATION OF DIVINE GRACE.

To return to the main line of thought: The certain view of the salvation of those who die in infancy is a very delightful one. It is a sad fact—

* Rev. A. K. H. Boyd's *Leisure Hours in Town*, pp. 311, 312
† *Thorndale, or, The Conflict of Opinions.* By William Smith.

not a speculation, not a dogma originating in the
Bible, and for which it is responsible; the Bible
finds it in existence, and, to repair the effects of
it, proclaims a gracious salvation—it is a sad fact
that children are born into the world under the
influence of the Fall. "Until the law," declares
the great apostle to the Gentiles, "sin was in the
world; but sin is not imputed when there is no
law. Nevertheless, death reigned from Adam to
Moses, even over them that had not sinned after
the similitude of Adam's transgression." Rom. v.
14. This means that children suffer and die
before they have committed any actual offence
as Adam did. And this is indisputable. We see
the proof of it every day. The infant a month
or a week old writhes in the arms of its nurse,
and then is laid in the grave before it has committed the first moral act. Multitudes of children
thus die early, while those who grow up begin
to sin, as soon as they commence to act at all,
and enter upon a career of greater or less suffering. If, then, God's gracious plan of redemption
is such that, while none who reach the age of
moral agency can be saved without faith and
repentance, receiving thereby actively the righteousness of Christ, those who die in infancy,

through the connection of the first great sin with the race, shall, as a provision of the Father's covenant with the Son, have the Redeemer's righteousness imputed to them, and be fitted for the glorious abodes of holiness through the almighty influence of the Spirit, transforming the moral character, removing the disposition to sin with which all are born and which so soon begins to manifest itself, and implanting the seed of holiness, which shall at once spring up and bloom forth in the holy service of heaven,—does it not in a remarkable manner manifest the grace of God ? Is it not the crowning proof of the assertion, "Where sin abounded, grace did much more abound; that as sin hath reigned unto death, even so might grace reign through righteousness unto eternal life by Jesus Christ our Lord"? Rom. v. 21.

"That the benefits of redemption shall far outweigh the evils of the Fall is here clearly asserted. This we can in a measure comprehend, because—1. The number of the saved shall doubtless greatly exceed the number of the lost. Since the half of mankind die in infancy, and, according to the Protestant doctrine, are heirs of salvation, and since in the future state of the

Church the knowledge of the Lord is to cover the earth, we have reason to believe that *the lost shall bear to the saved no greater proportion than the inmates of a prison do to the mass of the community.* 2 Because the eternal Son of God, by his incarnation and mediation, exalts his people to a far higher state of being than our race if unfallen could ever have attained. 3 Because the benefits of redemption are not to be confined to the human race. Christ is to be admired in his saints. It is through the Church that the manifold wisdom of God is to be revealed throughout all ages to principalities and powers. The redemption of man is to be the great source of knowledge and blessedness to the intelligent universe." *

ANSWER TO SKEPTICAL OBJECTION.

Behold what an answer we have here to an objection drawn from the discoveries of modern astronomy! Once it was supposed that the earth was the most important part of the universe, and that the sun, the moon and the stars were made for it and were dependent upon it. They wor-

* Dr. Charles Hodge's *Commentary on Romans* (on v. 20), p. 279, unabridged edition.

shiped it as in Joseph's dream they worshiped
him. The earth was the centre of creation. But
the telescope has revealed the fact that, compared
with the other worlds which unceasingly roll on
through the infinite space, our earth is an insig-
nificant ball. So small a part of the universe is
our whole solar system that it has been compared
to a little boat rocking on the great waves of the
universal ether. Look at the fixed stars. "If the
whole planetary system were lighted up into a
globe of fire, it would exceed by many millions
of times the magnitude of this world, and yet
only appear a small lucid point from the nearest
of them. If a body were projected from the sun
with the velocity of a cannon-ball, it would take
hundreds of thousands of years before it described
that mighty interval which separates the nearest
of the fixed stars from our sun and from our
system. If this earth, which moves at more than
the inconceivable velocity of a million and a half
of miles a day, were to be hurried from its orbit,
and to take the same rapid flight over this immense track, it would not arrive at the termination of its journey after taking all the time which
has elapsed since the creation of the world." *

* Chalmers's *First Astronomical Discourse.*

Beyond the orbit of Neptune, the outer planet of
our solar system, which is nearly three thousand
millions of miles from us, is a tremendous vacuity,
"the general depth of which is at least sixty
millions of millions of miles in every direction." *
Across that unimaginable empty space comes the
light of the so-called fixed stars. The nearest of
them is so far away that if we were to travel
toward it on a wave of light at the speed of nearly
twelve millions of miles a minute, it would take us
three years to reach it. "A railway-train, travel-
ing night and day at the rate of thirty-two miles
per hour, would take three hundred and forty-two
years and three months to reach the sun; and
since the nearest fixed star is 269,420 times more
distant, we could not reach it in less than ninety-
two million years." † Some of the stars of the
Milky Way, "itself but an island in the great
ocean of the universe," though containing twenty
millions of suns, are at such a remove from us
that their light takes five hundred years to reach
the earth. Farther off are nebulæ, thirty thousand years distant as the light travels; and others
as yet unresolvable by telescopes, fifty thousand

* Burr's *Ecce Cœlum*

† Luthardt's *Fundamental Truths of Christianity*, p 89.

years away; and others still, it is asserted, twenty million years.

These numbers are astounding. We cannot comprehend them. Well, compared with those innumerable orbs which roll through that infinite space, our earth is in size only a point, "a dot." Therefore has the objector to Christianity said,* It is an extravagance and a weakness to suppose that God would make so much of this "grain of sand in the sea of his universe," and of its puny inhabitants, as to devise for them a stupendous plan of salvation which necessitated the incarnation and death of his own Son! Incredible that such a wonderful work should be done for the benefit of this world, and of this world alone, when if it were blotted from existence it would not be missed! Still more incredible when the Bible represents that but a small portion of the inhabitants of the earth are saved by this marvelous scheme!

But the objection belittles God. It assumes that special attention to a part of his creation would be inconsistent with his general supervision of the whole; whereas the Infinite can notice the fall of every tiny sparrow without having his

* In a spirit far diffe ent from that of the psalmist in Ps. viii.

attention distracted from any other part of his kingdom.*   Moreover, it takes for granted that the earth alone is affected by the incarnation and death of the Son of God; whereas the work of redemption has an influence on the universe which only eternity can disclose.†   And, further,

* Addison has in *The Spectator* a fine number (565), in which he deals with this point, contrasting himself with the universe, and meeting the error that God's attention to the infinitely great would preclude the special oversight of individuals. The error is an outgrowth of "the poorness of our conceptions" of God until they are remedied by further reflection. "We ourselves cannot attend to many different objects at the same time. . . . When, therefore, we reflect on the divine nature, we are so used and accustomed to this imperfection in ourselves that we cannot forbear in some measure ascribing it to Him in whom there is no shadow of imperfection." In that paper Addison has a forcible comparison which is made stronger by the wonderful astronomical discoveries that have been made since his day: "Were the sun, which enlightens this part of creation, with all the host of planetary worlds that move about him, utterly extinguished and annihilated, they would not be missed more than a grain of sand upon the sea-shore. The space they possess is so exceedingly little in comparison of the whole that it would scarce make a blank in creation. The chasm would be imperceptible to an eye that could take in the whole compass of Nature and pass from one end of the creation to the other; *as it is possible there may be such in ourselves hereafter* or in creatures which are at present more exalted than ourselves."

† "It must be regarded as a narrow and unbiblical theory

it detracts from the numerical results of salvation.
One human soul is worth more than the largest
world of matter;* and if the saved were few, their

which limits the whole effects of the atonement to man. . . .
It will be found that our Lord constantly spoke with his eye
upon all the relations of the universe, and with the consciousness
that his work had a reference to them all. . . . In a word, it is
the central fact of God's present procedure or moral rule in the
universe, and that on which all depends."—Smeaton's *Our
Lord's Doctrine of the Atonement*, pp 283, 284. "The question
as to the relation which the incarnation upon earth bears to the
spiritual inhabitants of other worlds coincides with that as to the
relation between the creation of man and that of these spiritual
beings . . . If it is lawful to regard man as the microcosm—*i. e.*
as the representative of every creature, and the being who in
himself combines all substances, potencies and capabilities of
body and soul which are scattered throughout the universe—we
can also conceive how God, when he assumed the nature of man,
had thereby also in a certain sense taken upon himself the nature
of all other creatures. The fall and rebellion of part of the
angels had introduced a schism into the worlds of other spiritual beings; it had destroyed the harmony of the universe. To
restore it man was created, and, when he fell, redeemed, because
he was capable of redemption Hence the incarnation upon
earth was of advantage to the entire universe."—Kurtz's *History
of the Old Covenant*, 2, xcv and xcvi.

* Some of my readers may remember the magnificent peroration of Griffin's sermon on *The Kingdom of Christ*, which
bursts out with this sentence : "Standing, as I now do, in sight
of a dissolving universe, beholding the dead arise, the world in
flames, the heavens fleeing away, all nations convulsed with

rescue would be worthy of the sacrifice. But when, in the light in which we now look at their number, the redeemed of all ages down to the last hour shall be gathered home to heaven, they may present an array of happy immortals beside which the aggregate even of the starry worlds shall dwindle into littleness.

THE MILLENNIAL MULTITUDE.

3. The force of this assertion will be increased by recurring to, and amplifying, a remark which has been already made. With the immense multitude of the infant redeemed from generation to generation we must associate the myriads of an age that is yet to come, during which the number of saved adults shall be greatly multiplied. Vagaries are frequently indulged in as to the millennium. Many carnal and unscriptural notions are propagated about it. Theories are advanced which almost bring the name itself into disrepute. But this must not drive us from the delightful scriptural statements.

A period is coming in the history of the world—and it shall be a long-continued one—when the

terror or rapt in the vision of the Lamb, I pronounce the conversion of a single pagan of more value than all the wealth that ever Omnipotence produced."

gospel of Jesus shall have free course and be glorified to an extent that has never yet been witnessed. The knowledge of the Lord shall run to
and fro through the earth. Every nation shall
possess it. The kingdom of Christ shall extend
over all lands. The whole world shall be at peace.
Truth and righteousness shall everywhere be in
the ascendant. Temporal prosperity shall bless
the Church and the earth alike. There shall be
a far greater number of truly-converted and holy
persons in the world than during any previous period of its history. And this because it shall be
a time of the most wonderful working of the Holy
Spirit. The extent of this is indicated in Scripture by very expressive figures : "I will pour water
upon him that is thirsty, and floods upon the dry
ground; I will pour my Spirit upon thy seed, and
my blessing upon thine offspring, and they shall
spring up as among the grass, as willows by the
watercourse. One shall say, I am the Lord's, and
another shall call himself by the name of Jacob,
and another shall subscribe with his hand unto
the Lord, and surname himself by the name
of Israel." Isa. xliv. 3–5. The number of the
saved and the rapidity with which they will come
to Christ shall justify the exclamation, "Who are

these that fly as a cloud, and as the doves to their
windows?" Isa. lx. 8. The unbelieving Jews shall
be turned to the Messiah. The forces of the Gentiles shall come in such streams that the gates
shall be open continually; they shall not be shut
night or day. That will be a glorious time for the
Church of God. It shall immensely increase the
number of the saved. Add the believers of that
period to the host of true adult Christians and of
the infant redeemed in all previous ages, and the
trophies of our divine Redeemer's power may be
such as to astonish men themselves, send a quiver
of mortification through the ranks of our spiritual
enemies, and give the angels, in their rejoicing
over saved souls, notes of praise that shall be
heard through all heaven, and from star to star
through a space that is infinite in its extent.

THE NARROW PATH.

4. This view of the completed number of the
redeemed magnifies the grace of God It wonderfully intensifies our conception of the far-
reaching influence of the work of our blessed
Lord. But the enrapturing and comforting color
of the heavenly vision must be shaded by a prac-

tical truth which is of deep personal interest to hearers and readers of the gospel.

In the apocalyptic picture "the wall of the city had twelve foundations, and in them the names of the twelve apostles of the Lamb." V. 14. This reminds us of the passage in the Epistle to the Ephesians in which Paul compares the redeemed to a temple: "Now, therefore, ye are no more strangers and foreigners, but fellow-citizens with the saints and of the household of God; and are built upon the foundation of the apostles and prophets, Jesus Christ himself being the chief cornerstone; in whom all the building fitly framed together groweth unto an holy temple in the Lord; in whom ye also are builded together for an habitation of God through the Spirit." Eph. ii. 19–22.

The new Jerusalem is the city of the redeemed. Their salvation is built upon the precious truth of God as revealed by Christ and made known to us through his prophets and apostles. On that truth the city and its inhabitants for ever stand. Through the reception of that truth, and obedience to it, men must enter the city. And the Master has left on record one declaration which, with startling directness, limits the number of the redeemed, and exhibits the way that must be entered upon and persevered in by those who shall at the last be found among the glorified.

"Are there few that be saved?" he was once asked. He gave no direct reply to the inquiry, though in other portions of the inspired volume the answer is found as we have exhibited it. Perhaps perceiving that the motive which prompted the inquirer was a wrong one, or that the question was based upon the restricted Jewish idea of redemption, the great Teacher urged those who surrounded him to make sure of their own salvation by agonizing to enter in at the strait gate. The entrance is difficult. Many that expect to enter shall fail, to their eternal sorrow and confusion. Many others of whom you know nothing shall appear among the number of the saved, for they shall come from the east, and from the west, and from the north, and from the south, and shall sit down in the kingdom of God. Your position as Jews according to the flesh (he tells his hearers) will not save you eternally. Your presence near to God in your earthly privileges is not enough. The gate is open now, but it is very narrow. Agonize to enter it, for the hour is coming when it shall be shut, and no entreaty of yours can open it again. Then how fearful shall be your position, not only to find yourselves cut off from your fathers according to the flesh, but to know that Gentiles from all quarters of the globe, whom in your narrowness you exclude, have entered and are saved! Luke xiii. 23–30.

At an earlier period in his ministry our Lord had condensed the truth contained in that passage into a more startling form: "Enter ye in at the strait gate; for wide is the gate and broad is the way that leadeth to destruction, and many there be which go in thereat; because strait is the gate and narrow is the way which leadeth unto life, and few there be that find it." Matt. vii. 13, 14.

In the East, cities were entered through passes, at the beginning not at the close of which were the gates. Travelers first went through the gate, and then entered upon the path or road which led into the city. There were broad roads, and there were narrow roads. There were wide gates, and there were strait * gates. Under this form the Saviour depicts the course of the human race. Over our world are two ways. One leads down to destruction. The other leads up to life. The one that leads to destruction is broad, and its

---

* *Strait,* that is, narrow—not *straight* in opposition to crooked

8

gate wide. The other is narrow, and the gate of entrance to it strait. And the sad fact is, that the multitude are on the broad road; "many go in thereat." It is conspicuous and easy of access. The consequence is, that the masses find their way into it. The narrow way to heaven, however, is not only difficult of entrance when discovered, but it is not even discovered by the greater number. "Few there be that find it."

The entrance upon the narrow path involves the exercise of painful self-denial.* Sinful lusts, evil dispositions, unholy inclinations must be pressed down, forced out, left behind. The way to destruction is broad, because it is the way of fallen nature. Sin has smoothed it and made it easy for men to travel upon. They go thereon easily, because illicit pleasure lures and their sins may have full sway over them. The narrow way is avoided by many, because they love their vices too well to be willing to press them down and force them away from themselves. And the gate is too narrow to permit sins to be taken in thereat.

* The word *narrow* means pressed, contracted, and it suggests the idea of a difficult as well as inconvenient entrance. It is the root of the noun which in Acts xiv. 22 is translated *tribulation:* "We must through much tribulation enter into the kingdom of God."

This is the only thing which ever keeps the number of the saved among the living, active, throbbing men of any generation apparently small. Nothing but a voluntary persistence in sin bars any from the bliss of the eternally saved.

There are some points connected with the extent of redemption, God's electing love and the Holy Spirit's power over souls with which theologians have made very free, but which no finite mind can now clearly explain. If we could read the completed work as seen from the divine throne, I doubt not it would appear that

> "God hath done all
> That even God can do to save lost man,
> Unless he take from him conscience, free-will,
> Knowledge and faith, those precious, priceless gifts,
> And force him, like a bridled mule, by dint
> Of whip and spur, to keep the narrow way
> Which leads to life eternal."   .

The sorrowfully-indignant question which he addressed to his ancient people has a wider application: "What could have been done more to my vineyard that I have not done in it?" Isa. v. 4.

Eternal life is the free gift of God, through the Lord Jesus Christ, to dying sinners. The worst and vilest may have it. It is not refused to the

most helpless, and it is received by a simple act
of faith.   But to believe in the first place, and to
persevere in the faith afterward, involve a complete transformation of the nature and a renun-
ciation of sin which narrow the way of life.   They
who go in at the strait gate must approach it
with the humility, the teachableness, the docility
of children : "Except ye be converted and become
as little children, ye cannot enter the kingdom of
heaven." Matt. xviii. 3.   They must come with
heart-grief on account of sin, and with sincere and
persistent effort to give up even the most cherished
of their vicious habits : "Repent and be converted,
that your sins may be blotted out." Acts iii. 19.
"Except ye repent ye shall all perish." Luke xiii.
3.   And to repent is not merely to be afraid of the
punishment, the woes, the pains which follow sins
that have been committed, but to be sorry for them,
and to grieve over and hate them, because they are
against the holy and the loving God, and to struggle with the whole might against them in all the
future; for gospel repentance has its foundation in
a radical change in the nature, which more or less
quickly manifests itself in the complete outgrow-
ing of holiness of life, so that of the narrow way
itself it may be said, "A highway shall be there,

and a way, and it shall be called the way of holiness; the unclean shall not pass over it." Isa. xxxv.
8. Those who enter upon it and walk over it
toward the glory of heaven must deny the most
darling lusts or vicious desires of the flesh. They
must renounce all iniquities: "They that are
Christ's have crucified the flesh with the affections
and lusts." Gal. v. 24. Our sins put Christ to
death; receiving his salvation and entering upon
life eternal, we must in turn put to death those
sins. "If any man will come after me," cries the
Redeemer as he goes himself through this world
and leads in the path to heaven, "let him deny
himself, and take up his cross daily and follow
me." Luke ix. 23.

What are the sins which must be crucified?
The apostle presents a catalogue of some of
them: "The works of the flesh are manifest,
which are these: adultery, fornication, uncleanness, lasciviousness, envyings, idolatry, witchcraft,
hatred, variance, emulations, wrath, strife, sedi-
tions, heresies, murders, drunkenness, revelings,
and such like; of the which I tell you before, as
I have also told you in time past, that they which
do such things shall not inherit the kingdom of
God." Gal. v. 19–21. A fearful brood, truly, and

there are none that have been free from them all.
They are pleasant to the flesh, and they crowd
the broad road to destruction with travelers. But
in the way of life eternal they must be crucified;
deep repentance for their commission must be exercised; and the desire to be delivered perfectly
from them must prevail, though for a long time,
in the struggle between them and the new nature,
they may obtain temporary triumphs. Those
who are living in the deliberate practice of any
of them, or of similar acts of the flesh, are not in
the way to heaven. On the other hand, some of
the positive characteristics of the narrow path are
" love, joy, peace, long-suffering, gentleness, goodness, faith, meekness, temperance." Gal. v. 22.
They who are in that path exhibit all these graces
in some degree, and desire to possess them more
perfectly. Day by day they must wish for perfect
holiness (2 Cor. xiii 9), and earnestly strive after
it, and mourn over their failure to reach it.

Moreover, the narrow way is a life of singularity.
It is a departure from the world, from its customs,
its maxims, its modes of living, its objects. The
call of God is, " Come out from among them, and
be ye separate." 2 Cor vi. 17. " Be not conformed
to this world, but be ye transformed by the renew-

ing of your mind." Rom. xii. 2. Between the
ways of piety and the ways of the world there
is an irreconcilable antagonism. "Love not the
world, neither the things that are in the world.
If any man love the world, the love of the Father
is not in him. For all that is in the world, the
lust of the flesh, and the lust of the eyes, and
the pride of life, is not of the Father, but is of
the world." 1 John ii. 15–17. This develops to
a greater or less degree, and in different forms, a
spirit of opposition and hatred to the truly pious.
The words of the Redeemer are, "If ye were of
of the world, the world would love his own; but
because ye are not of the world, but I have chosen
you out of the world, therefore the world hateth
you. Remember the word that I said unto you,
The servant is not greater than his lord. If they
have persecuted me, they will also persecute you:
if they have kept my saying, they will keep yours
also." John xv. 19, 20.

The way to heaven continues as narrow as is
the gate through which it is entered upon. The
moral law of God is no longer a covenant of life,
on perfect obedience to which by us is conditioned
our eternal happiness: Christ has fulfilled that
condition for his people. But they are still bound

.by it as a rule of life; and Jesus has expounded it as stricter in its spirit than in its letter. "So far from intending to pare away Moses' tables, he carries every commandment to its utmost extent. A wanton look is declared to be adultery, and a wrathful heart is deemed murder, and the man who calls his neighbor a fool is threatened with hell-fire." It is a gospel declaration, too, that if a man should keep the whole law, and yet offend in one point, he is guilty of all. James ii. 10. All this requires continued watchfulness and prayer-fulness and strife against temptation on the part of Christ's own people as they walk toward heaven; for want of which too many, who appeared to have entered the strait gate, fall away and show that they have never really done so. The true believer is under the necessity of daily struggling against tendency and temptation, to keep in the path. If, on the one side, he believe in the doctrine of the final perseverance of the truly regenerate, he knows, on the other, that this is made sure to him only by overcoming sin in its various forms. He has room to feel anxious enough about his own position to keep him as careful every minute as he was when first he believed. He sees lukewarm professors, formalists, backsliders, all around him : is he, may he be, one of them ? *

Reader, in which way are you ? You cannot enter heaven without a holy nature manifesting itself in faith, repentance and loving obedience to the Lord. Have you it ? Are you exhibiting its evidences ?

The great city shall be filled with inhabitants. Its incalculable number of mansions shall be occupied. But what if you should not be among them ? Prevent the possibility of that by an immediate entrance through the strait gate into the narrow way, and be faithful therein unto death, that you may receive the crown of life.

* How alarming the words with which Bunyan closes his *Pilgrim's Progress!* After seeing Christian and Hopeful pass through the opened gate, he turns and beholds Ignorance, who, with much confidence and comfort, though without the true title of faith, had crossed the dark river and demanded admission; but " Then I saw that there was a way to hell even from the gates of heaven, as well as from the City of Destruction !"

III.

CHRIST'S TRANSFIGURATION · THE DEVOTIONAL LIFE.

THE transfiguration of our Redeemer (Matt. xvii. 1–13; Mark ix. 2–13; Luke ix. 28–36) opened to earth a temporary glimpse of the glory of heaven. As beheld by the three favored apostles who were taken up to it, and as recorded by the inspired pens for all ages, it illustrates and enforces some important lessons in reference to the life here as a preparation for the life hereafter. In that view I shall consider it.

THE TIME AND CIRCUMSTANCES OF THE TRANSFIGURATION.

We have sometimes seen the heavens, as the day was sinking into evening, lighted up with peculiar splendor. An expanse of leaden cloud, broken now and then into brightness, had arched

122

the earth since the morning and given a sombre
hue to the face of creation The sun had been
behind the clouds, but concealed from view. His
light had been beaming through the watery sea
overhead, but tinged with darkness and gloom.
Just before his descent beneath the horizon, however, the clouds broke away and his rays bathed
the vast concave in a glory that was unutterable.
The deep blue, an ocean of light unfathomable,
spread itself everywhere behind the rifted clouds,
which, like innumerable islets of gold, seemed to
have their shores laved by the mighty ocean and
to lie sluggishly in its calm waters, while the rays
of light which poured down through them and
past them clothed the green of earth in a charming and luxuriant softness. Above, around, everywhere, the sun vindicated his power as the king
of day. His majesty had only been concealed

Our Lord Jesus Christ was approaching the
evening of his earthly life. He had been in the
form of God, and thought it not robbery to be
equal with God. His glory had filled all heaven.
But when he made himself of no reputation, and
took upon him the form of a servant, and was
made in the likeness of men, that glory passed
under a cloud. Its full brightness did not illumine

the earth.   The plains of Bethlehem were bathed
in it on the night when the brightness of the Lord
shone round the shepherds and heralded the
miraculous birth.   It rested strangely for a little
while over the Jordan at his baptism.   Its power
in the perfect purity of a holy life, the wisdom of
divine words, the wonderful exhibition of miraculous energy, appeared to the purged eyes of the
pure in heart.   The full orb, however, was concealed from view.   But on the Mount of Transfiguration it burst forth with the magnificence of
heaven.   The Redeemer would not descend to the
grave enveloped in darkness.   He would not leave
his chosen few without an entrancing sight of his
divine majesty.   Therefore, though the veil of his
humanity was not removed, though the clouds
were there still, the God of the universe shone
through them with a brightness which the morning of his earthly life had not exhibited, and
which rested upon the cross, and with the golden
splendor of the glorious land rimmed the cloud
of darkness that was there.   It showed that the
Son of God, after his contact with sin, would go
back to the capital of his empire deprived of none
of his brilliancy, but still able to enlighten all
worlds and all systems.

THE SPLENDOR OF THE TRANSFIGURATION.

With the mysteries of the event I do not pro-
pose specially to deal. Nor shall I dwell on its
theological import. I shall bring out some of the
minor lessons that are suggested by its surrounding circumstances, and are connected with our
spiritual life now. But, before passing to them,
gaze for a little while on the exceeding splendor
of the scene itself.

The descriptions of it are multiplied by the
inspired writers in order to intensify in our minds
the conception of its brilliancy. On a high mountain, to which our Lord had withdrawn with three
of his disciples, he was transfigured. This was
not a change of person, "such as to destroy his
visible identity, but merely a transcendent dignity and splendor." Under it "the fashion of his
countenance was altered," and "his face did shine
as the sun." "It was lighted up not alone, as the
face of Moses once was, by the lingering reflection
of the outward glory upon which it had gazed, but
illumined from within, as if the hidden glory was
bursting through the fleshly veil and kindling it into
radiance as it passed." * The divine glory which

* " Putting all the accounts together, it would appear that the
light shone not *upon* him *from without*, but *out of him from*

dwelt within, and which at a later period, when he spake from heaven to Saul of Tarsus on the high-road to Damascus, shone down upon earth with a brightness exceeding the noonday sun, then pierced through the earthly human nature and wrapped the mountain also in its brilliancy. Bathed in it, even his raiment became " white as the light," " white and glistering," or, as Mark has it, simply " shining;" but the original word there, as used by Greek writers, is exceedingly suggestive. By one it is applied to the glistering of polished metallic surfaces and to the glittering of arms; by another to the twinkling of the stars; and by another still to the flashing of lightning.   Mark adds that it was " exceeding white as snow." "The word means, originally, *clear* and *bright*, as applied by Homer to pure water, the sense of color being secondary and indefinite, comprehending a variety of shades from gray to pure white." Here it expresses an " effulgent white light, without shade or spot," a pure bright whiteness such as earth cannot produce.

We have beheld a regiment of soldiers marching along the streets, with their brightly-polished

within · he was all irradiated; it was one blaze of dazzling, celestial glory; it was himself glorified."—*Brown* on Luke ix. 29.

muskets and bayonets glittering in the noonday sun, and we recollect how dazzling to our eyes was the sight On a clear, cold wintry night, when the stars shone at their brightest, we have looked up and seen them twinkling in their brilliant purity. On a dark and stormy night we have seen the terrible lightning flash through the darkness, and we remember how blinding it was. On a winter day, after a fall of snow which had covered the earth with its garment, we have seen the sun come out clear and shining, and we know how difficult it was with open eyes to walk over the white carpet.

All these comparisons, however, give us but a faint idea of the brilliancy with which the Redeemer's transfiguration invested even his garments. More than sixty years afterward the beloved John must have remembered the scene when, in apocalyptic vision, he looked into that heaven the glory of which had rested upon the mountain, and the ascended Lord thus appeared to him: " One like unto the Son of man, clothed with a garment down to the foot, and girt about the paps with a golden girdle. His head and his hairs were white like wool, as white as snow; and his eyes were as a flame of fire;

and his feet like unto fine brass, as if they burned
in a furnace, and his voice as the sound of many
waters. And he had in his right hand seven
stars; and out of his mouth went a sharp two-
edged sword, and his countenance was as the sun
shineth in his strength." Rev i. 13–16.* The
Lord was then in heaven, and the effect of his
glorious appearance was that the enraptured apostle fell at his feet as dead. This scene on the
mount was heaven let down to earth for a little
while.

Something more splendid it was than our globe
ever witnessed before or since.

---

* " This description of the glorified Lord, sublime as a purely
mental conception, but intolerable if we were to give it an outward form and expression, . . . sublime and majestic as it is,
is only such so long as we keep it wholly apart from any external embodiment. Produce it outwardly—the sword going forth
from the mouth, the eyes as a flame of fire, the hair white as
wool, the feet as molten brass—and each and all of these
images violate more or less our sense of beauty Bengel, miss-
ing this important distinction, has sought to give a picture of
the Lord Jesus according to this description, prefixing it to
his German commentary on the Apocalypse—a picture which is
almost degrading, and only not deeply offensive to every feeling
of reverence and awe because we know that it was not so
intended by this admirable man."—Trench on *The Epistles to the
Seven Churches*, pp. 64, 65.

The three disciples were asleep when the transfiguration commenced, for it was probably at night, and they were weary with the ascent of the mountain. Under the pressure of their fatigue their eyes grew heavy until they closed, leaving their Master engaged in prayer. But the brilliant light falling upon their eyelids soon aroused them. Then they beheld not only the transfigured form of the Lord, but two other glorious appearances. Elijah and Moses had come from heaven to commune with the Great Prophet about the consummation of his redemption work. They were really on the mount that night in sight of the three apostles. It was no dream, no vision, no apparition in the sense of an "appearance without substance." The impression which it made was so vivid that thirty years afterward, Peter, writing of it, declared, "We have not followed cunningly devised fables* when we made known unto you the power and coming of our Lord Jesus Christ, but were eye-witnesses of his majesty. For he received from God the Father honor and glory when there came such a voice to

* "Many," says Farrar (in his *Life of Christ*, ii. 30), "have resolved the narrative of the transfiguration into a myth; it is remarkable that in this verse St. Peter *is expressly repudiating the very kind of myths* (μῦθοι σεσοφισμένοι) under which this would be classed."

him from the excellent glory, This is my beloved Son, in whom I am well pleased. And this voice which came from heaven we heard when we were with him in the holy mount." 2 Pet. i. 16.

Nine hundred years before, Elijah had gone to heaven. Without passing through death, his corruptible body had changed into the incorruptible, his mortal had put on immortality, and "in that transfigured form he stood beside the transfigured form of Jesus." Five hundred and fifty years earlier still Moses had died, though no man knew his tomb, for the Lord buried him. How he appeared on the mount we cannot tell—whether "provided with a temporary or apparent body, like the angels who descended to the earth in patriarchal times, or whether, by an anticipation of the final resurrection, he was clothed already with the body which he is to wear for ever." * But they were both really on the mount with their Lord, and the witnesses were enabled to recognize them and to understand their conversation with Jesus.

ITS PRIMARY LESSONS.

What a significancy there was in the selection

* This and the preceding brief quotations in this section are from Dr. Addison Alexander's *Commentary on Mark, in locis*

of those two from the long line of Old Testament characters for appearance at this magnificent revelation of heaven! As at the beginning of his ministry Jesus spent forty days in the wilderness, so Moses and Elijah had spent forty days and forty nights in the Mount of God. They spoke of the decease which he was to accomplish at Jerusalem, as Luke tells us, or, as it is more strictly, his "exode," his exodus or departure in his redemption work, a great fact which had been typified ages before, in its saving effect upon his people, by the exodus of Moses from Egypt at the head of Israel, and by the exodus of Elijah, in the glorious termination of his work, from Elisha, with a chariot of fire and horses of fire by a whirlwind into heaven. Their presence testified to the fact that the law and the prophets were fulfilled in Jesus, for through Moses the law was given, and Elijah was the great prophet who restored it in the ten tribes in the days of their apostasy On the mount they paid their homage to Him who was the great Lawgiver.

For the apostles there was a volume of instruction contained in the vision. Their Master had been living a poor wanderer on the earth; here the glory of heaven is his, and two of the greatest of

its inhabitants come to honor him, though he was
despised by the world.   He had been trampling
on the human additions to the law, and giving occasion to his enemies to charge that he was de-
stroying the law itself; here he stands between the
inspired revealer and the restorer of that law, showing its fulfillment in him, and receiving honor from
those who had maintained it.   His life was not
out of communion with theirs.   He had shortly
before told his followers of the ignominious death
to which he was going; in glory the representatives of heaven discourse of it as a foreordained
thing for man's redemption and for the Redeemer's glorification.   They did not stumble at the
cross; therefore neither need the disciples.   To
crown the whole, renewed testimony is given by
the Father to the truth of Christ's claims and renewed approval is expressed of his great mission:
" This is my beloved Son, in whom I am well
pleased."   All this had its place in the educational
discipline of the apostles for their peculiar work in
their peculiar time.

   The foregoing are the truths which are generally presented when the vision is considered.
But under them, and in connection with the way
in which they were communicated, there are some

other lessons that have a permanent bearing on our spiritual life.

THE DIVINE CHOICE OF BELIEVERS.

1. It illustrates the fact that there is a divine choice of some of the members of the Church of God to peculiar privileges in heaven as well as on earth.

Jesus took up to the Mount of Transfiguration only Peter and James and John. From the larger number of his disciples it had pleased him to choose twelve who were to hold special communion with him until his death, and then have a peculiar honor and a peculiar responsibility in the reorganization of the Church. From those twelve he further selected these three, and made them his companions when he entered the room where the daughter of Jairus lay, here again at the transfiguration, and later still in the garden when he was bowed down by his awful agony. Yet again, of these three it was the peculiar privilege of John to recline upon his bosom at the Supper.

Why these various acts of choice? Because the three were possessed of particular mental gifts which, under the baptism of grace, would fit them for an important work in the Church of

Christ? If they had those gifts, he bestowed them in the beginning, and could have given them to others. Because they were to suffer the most, and it was meet that they should have a special preparation, and particularly this view of the transcendent glory of their Lord for whom they were to die? Perhaps so; for if we read their history aright they were the greatest sufferers among the apostles; so that their privileges were balanced by their trials. But that, too, was in God's hands. It was "Even so, Father, for so it seemed good in thy sight." Matt. xi. 26. All through life the hand and the voice of God appear, assigning to us our places, conferring upon us our privileges, preparing us for our various duties, and yet not taking away our responsibility, nor lessening the necessity for persistent activity on our part. He still favors some of his people with higher spiritual joys than others. The less favored have no right to complain, nor ought the more favored to be unduly elated, lest they fall as Peter afterward did

"There are three great principles in life which weave its warp and woof, apparently incompatible with each other, yet they harmonize, and, in their blending, create this strange life of ours. The first

is, our fate is in our own hands, and our blessedness or misery is the exact result of our own
acts The second is, 'there's a divinity that shapes
our ends, rough-hew them as we will.' The third
is, the race is not to the swift, nor the battle to the
strong, but time and chance happen to them all
Accident, human will, the shaping will of the
Deity,—these things make up life. Or rather, perhaps, we see a threefold causality from some
defect in our spiritual eyesight. Could we see
as He sees, all would be referable to one principle
which would contain them all, as the simple,
single law of gravitation embraces the complex
phenomena of the universe; and as, on the other
hand, by pressing the eyeballs, so as to destroy
their united impression, you may see all things
double." *

The Lord gives the mount of exaltation as a
preparation for the valley of conflict. This leads
to another teaching of the vision.

THE PREPARATION OF BELIEVERS FOR TRIALS.

2. It strikingly illustrates the kindness of the
Lord in preparing his people for the tribulations
that are to beat upon them.

* F. W. Robertson's *Sermons*, i. 295, 296

Doubtless, this had a strengthening influence upon our Redeemer himself. " We know too little of the inner history and of the human mind of the man Jesus to say how seasonable, how serviceable, this brief translation into the society of the upper sanctuary may have been—this solemn announcement of his Sonship by his Father—what treasures this declaration of satisfaction with all his earthly work, of strength and of counsel fitting him for the approaching hour and power of darkness, may have conveyed into his soul. Doubtless, here, too, there were purposes of mercy and grace toward the Redeemer thus subserved which it is difficult for us to apprehend, more difficult for us fully to fathom." * We can, however, see the influence clearly in the case of the disciples.

Only a few days before, Jesus had given them the first formal prediction of his coming death at Jerusalem: "From that time forth, Jesus began to show unto his disciples how that he must go unto Jerusalem, and suffer many things of the elders and chief priests and scribes, and be killed, and be raised again the third day." Matt. xvi. 21. The apostles could not understand this. Peter,

* *Sunday Magazine,* iii. 843.

the rash and the presumptuous, even had the temerity to rebuke Jesus for the saying. The event would be a sore trial of their faith. The time was approaching. And now, to sustain them under it, amid the glory of heaven two of the celestial inhabitants appear conversing with their Lord on this very subject. This, in connection with the renewed testimony which the Father bears to the Sonship of Jesus, shows the disciples that the death is necessarily connected with the work which their Lord had to perform, and would not in any degree mar the truth of his claims. The whole scene was specially designed to prepare them for the terrible catastrophe. Its message to them was: Be not cast down when ye see me buffeted and crucified. Under the darkness of Calvary's cross remember the bright vision of this mount. When ye hear me cry out, "My God, my God, why hast thou forsaken me?" remember the Father's declaration, "This is my beloved Son." And then be not faithless, but believing.

Furthermore, the life of the apostles was to be a life of suffering for their Master. Here, however, they have a glimpse of the glory to which their afflictions shall translate them. Here is

heaven before them—heaven come down to earth ;
here two of the worthies of old, who, after lives
of peculiar self-denial in the service of God, had
been taken home to glory—here already in the
brightness of the better land.   And the disciples
themselves shall be like them when they pass
through the gate of the grave.   How, then, can
they dread persecution and pain and death when
just beyond the river is the heaven from which
Moses and Elias had come, and where all the
departed redeemed were bathed in the glory of
eternity ?

The saved enter heaven immediately when
they die, and they can there recognize and have
communion with each other and with their Lord :
this was a view of the future which the scene impressed on the minds of the apostles   In itself it
was strengthening to them, as it is to us.   The
glory after death is not postponed to a remote
future.   It shines now above us.   Let death come
to believers when and how it may, it at once introduces them to the place of perfect bliss.   The
conscious and active happiness of the saved is
not suspended until the resurrection ; but now,
even now, those who have been taken from the
earth are in the enjoyment of it   Death is ever

the instantaneous translation of the redeemed to it. "Absent from the body, present with the Lord." 2 Cor. v. 8.

As God dealt with the apostles, so he deals with his Church and with individual believers still. If, on the one hand, he follows seasons of great depression with special visitations of his mercy, he prepares, on the other hand, for sore trials by peculiar manifestations of his love. Believer, is there some affliction in store for you? Christ is waiting to give you the grace which will carry you safely through it. Up to the mount of communion with him, that you may hear his ravishing words and gaze upon his glory. There he will give you at least the renewed pledge of his affection, as the Father did to the Redeemer on the Mount of Transfiguration, in the declaration, "This is my beloved Son," and to the apostles in the assertion that he was well pleased with his work; and as Jesus himself did to them in the words, "Be not afraid." As God's assurance was, in itself, strength for them, so this same precious truth will be of unutterable consolation to you. If nothing more be vouchsafed, it will be a flowing stream of comfort to have borne in upon your mind, through close communion with the divine

Three in One and meditation upon his words, the delightful truth that God is ever love to you; and that even the troubles which may be before you are bathed in that love, as really as the death of the Redeemer, itself a sore darkness and grief, was his exodus from pain and punishment to unending glory and the securing of glory for us.

> " I cannot always trace the way
>   Where thou, Almighty One, dost move;
> But I can always, always, say
>   That God is love.
>
> " When Fear her chilling mantle flings
>   O er earth, my soul to heaven above,
> As to her sanctuary, springs,
>   For God is love
>
> " When mystery clouds my darkened path,
>   I'll check my dread, my doubts reprove;
> In this my soul sweet comfort hath,
>   That God is love.
>
> " The entanglement which restless thought,
>   Mistrust and idle reasoning wove
> Are thus unraveled and unwrought,
>   For God is love.
>
> " Yes, God is love!   A thought like this
>   Can every gloomy thought remove,
> And turn all tears, all woes, to bliss,
>   For God is love."

SECRET COMMUNION WITH CHRIST NECESSARY.

3. This vision further illustrates the fact that in order thus to be strengthened for the conflicts of the life here, and to anticipate the life of heaven, we must frequently withdraw from the busy haunts of the world and have seasons of secret communion with Christ.

It was not in the streets of Jerusalem, nor by the wayside where the people were passing to and fro in the eager pursuit of business, nor even in the room where were gathered together all the members of the Church, that the glory of heaven came down upon the three disciples, and they saw such a thrilling sight and heard such ravishing words. "Jesus leadeth them up into a high mountain, apart, by themselves ; and he was trans-figured before them." *Apart by themselves !*

It was the Saviour's habit frequently to retire into secret places for solitary communion with the Father. He spent whole nights in prayer. Even *he* needed to divide his time, suspend his active labors, silence his tongue, and through quiet thoughtfulness be strengthened from above. He was in no haste to enter upon his public life. Thirty years were passed in obscurity and in unnoticed preparation before he commenced his

labors. And then there was many a suspension
of his public toils " No soul can preserve the
bloom and delicacy of its existence without lonely
musing and silent prayer; and the greatness of
this necessity is in proportion to the greatness
of the soul. There were many times during our
Lord's ministry when, even from the loneliness
of desert places he dismissed his most faithful
and beloved, that he might be yet more alone " *
As he approached the culmination of his work
he especially required this. The conflict in the
quiet and dark Gethsemane was a strengthening season for the gloom and the pain of
Calvary.

This element of the religious life is also made
very prominent in the other characters of the
Bible. It forms one of the most salient parts of
the description which is given in the first Psalm
of the righteous man: " His delight is in the law
of the Lord ; and in his law doth he meditate day
and night." At one of the critical periods in the
life of Isaac, the gentle, perhaps rather negative,
patriarch appears before us meditating in the field
at the eventide. Gen. xxiv. 63 Not, however,
the passive but the most active and energetic men

* Farrar's *Life of Christ*, i. 100.

of the inspired history are particularly mentioned
as cultivating this habit. As Joshua entered upon
his great military mission of conquest and settle-
ment in the promised land, God gave him this
charge : " This book of the law shall not depart
out of thy mouth ; but thou shalt meditate therein
day and night, that thou mayest observe to do
according to all that is written therein : for then
thou shalt make thy way prosperous, and then
thou shalt do wisely." Josh. i. 8, 9. The Psalmist
had declared : " As for me, I will call upon God ;
and the Lord shall save me. Evening and morning and at noon will I pray and cry aloud, and he
shall hear my voice " (Ps. lv. 16, 17) ; and with
the heaviest cares pressing upon him, Daniel, the
statesman and the prophet, continued faithful in
that custom ; for when his enemies obtained the
decree which they expected would result in his
ruin, " he went into his house ; and his windows
being open in his chamber toward Jerusalem, he
kneeled upon his knees three times a day, and
prayed, and gave thanks before his God, *as he
did aforetime.*" Dan. v. 10. David was a man
of unceasing activity, wonderful energy and wide
public responsibilities and duties, but the Psalms
which he wrote, and those which were written in

imitation of his utterances, show the substratum
of his energetic life. They pulsate with contemplative meditation: " My soul shall be satisfied
as with marrow and fatness ; and my mouth shall
praise thee with joyful lips. when I remember
thee upon my bed, and meditate on thee in the
night watches. I will remember the works of the
Lord : surely I will remember thy wonders of
old. I will meditate also of all thy work, and
talk of thy doings. I will meditate in thy precepts, and have respect unto thy ways Let the
proud be ashamed, for they dealt perversely with
me without a cause, but I will meditate in thy
precepts. Oh, how love I thy law! it is my
meditation all the day Thou through thy com-
mandments hast made me wiser than mine enemies : for they are ever with me. How precious
are thy thoughts unto me, O God! How great is
the sum of them ! If I should count them, they
are more in number than the sand : when I awake
I am still with thee I remember the days of
old, I meditate on all thy works; I muse on the
work of thy hands I stretch forth my hands
unto thee : my soul thirsteth after thee as a
thirsty land." Ps. lxiii 5, 6; lxxvii 11, 12; cxix.
15, 78, 97, 98; cxxxix 17. 18; cxliii 11; 5, 6

In the regular and persistent habit of meditation upon the revealed truths of God, and of communion with him in prayer, the faithful worthies of old received comfort under their trials and discouragements, and were strengthened to do the great deeds which they accomplished for God. In addition to this, when any one was to be commissioned for a specially difficult, protracted and far-reaching enterprise, he was first driven aside from the world for a season of spiritual discipline. The forty years which Moses passed in Midian were a necessary preparation for his great life-work. Elijah's briefer exile in Horeb was for him a similar training.

What the inspired men of God, and what the divine Jesus himself needed, we need infinitely more.

No one can arrive at a high degree of piety who has not frequent seasons of retirement, when the world is shut out, friends are banished and God alone is near "The soul collects its mightiest forces by being thrown in upon itself, and coerced solitude matures the mental and moral character marvelously." Frequent and regular devotional exercises in the closet and in the sanctuary are essential for our religious growth and fruitfulness

NEGLECT OF MEDITATIVE PIETY.

Perhaps this touches one great defect in our current piety. It is too little meditative and contemplative. The age is intensely practical. The world is for money-making in the most rapid manner. An unceasing, harassing excitement quivers through the body politic. Men toil to death in the pursuit of riches. Money is their god. In their efforts to procure the comforts and luxuries of life, and to build up a fortune, they can scarcely take time to think of anything but business. The consequent drain on their time and mental powers interferes sadly with the spiritualizing elements of their nature.

We are an active people. The age is terribly energetic. The activity which impels our manufacturing and commercial interests also sweeps the Church along. It is for extension. Its peculiar aspect is missionary—reaching beyond, abroad, to gather in the masses and bring the world quickly to the Redeemer. Stand up for Jesus! Scatter the truth! Preach the gospel! Labor for the conversion of souls! Gather the young into the Sabbath-school! Increase the financial resources of the Church! These are the watchwords. Right, too, in their proper relations, they are. And men are measured, in this practical age, as to their usefulness, by their ability in accomplishing these objects.

But with this action there should be a greater union of solitude, self-scrutiny, reading and meditation, for our own highest comfort and growth in grace. It is intensely soul-injurious for any individual to be for ever in the pursuit of business, or in the midst of company, or in the excitement of social pleasure.* We need frequent seasons of quietness for our spiritual growth. Activity, even though it be in a religious line, develops only one side of our spiritual being. Quiet thought must do its work in subduing the soul, chastening its graces and preparing it for a holier activity. The holy sacrament of the Supper fails

* Cecil's words express a truth which ought to influence all·
"I feel all that I know and all that I teach will do nothing
for my soul if I spend my time, as some people do, in business
or company. My soul starves to death in the best company, and
God is often lost in prayers and ordinances. 'Enter into thy
closet,' said he, and 'shut thy door' Some words in Scripture
are very emphatical. 'Shut thy door' means much: it means,
Shut out not only nonsense, but business; not only the company
abroad, but the company at home; it means, Let thy poor soul
have a little rest and refreshment, and God have opportunity to
speak to thee in a still, small voice, or he will speak to thee in
thunder."

in one of its purposes if the communicant does not comply with the apostolic injunction to examine himself before going to the sacred board: " Let a man examine himself, and so let him eat of that bread and drink of that cup." 1 Cor. xi. 28.

" He that intends to attain to the more inward and spiritual things of religion," says À Kempis, " must with Jesus depart from the multitude and press of people. . . . If thou desirest true contrition of heart, enter into thy secret chamber and shut out the tumults of the world, as it is written, ' In your chambers be ye grieved.' * In thy chamber thou shalt find what abroad thou shalt often lose The more thou visitest thy chamber, the more thou wilt like it; the less thou comest thereunto, the more thou wilt loathe it. If in the beginning of thy conversion thou art content to remain in it, and keep to it well, it will afterward be to thee a dear friend and a most pleasant comfort." " Shut thy door upon thee, and call unto thee Jesus, thy beloved. Stay with him in thy closet; for thou shalt not find so great a peace anywhere else." " Seek a convenient time to retire into thyself, and meditate often upon God's loving-kindnesses " †

* Ps. iv. 4 (Vulgate).   † *The Imitation of Christ,* bk. 1. ch. 20.

COMMUNION WITH RELIGIOUS WRITERS.

We cannot now in such seasons see the glory of heaven as the favored apostles saw it Moses and Elijah, and the Lord himself, will not appear to our mortal eyes. But we can have communion with them through the inspired record of their words and deeds. In the silence of our own rooms we can hold sweet converse also with the other inspired men of God—with the sweet singer of Israel in his psalms, the evangelical prophet in his Old Testament gospel, John in his words of love and gorgeous visions, Paul in his burning words of heaven's logic. The holy and the good of all ages, too, may meet us there in their works and in their biographies ;*—men whose tone "was not

---

* As reading is so important for mental and spiritual development, it will be interesting to quote a statement made a few years ago by a French writer, Rosseuw St. Hilaire, which is a tribute to Protestantism, and shows how favored we are : " Wherever the Bible is not made the foundation-stone of education, of society and of every form of life, there is no literature for children or for the people. Look at Spain, Italy, and even France; in a word, at every country in which the Bible is not read ; nowhere is there any reading for the child or the laborer. In Germany and England, on the contrary, there exists a Christian children's and popular literature, in which, as in a mirror, the national spirit is clearly reflected " Hence with us the works are scattered thick

merely uprightness of character and high-minded-
ness, but communion, a strong sense of personal
and ever-living communion, with God besides;"
such as Augustine in his *Confessions,* Thomas
à Kempis in his *Imitation of Christ,* Bishop Hall
in his *Contemplations,* Baxter in his *Saints' Rest,*
Doddridge in his *Rise and Progress of Religion in
the Soul,* Alexander in his *Religious Experience.*

Intercourse with such ethereal spirits, through
the devotional books they have left us, has its
special uses.*   " The mower has always his whet-

as leaves in Vallambrosa, from which all ages and classes can
derive their mental regimen.

* Dr. Shedd, in his Introduction to *Augustine's Confessions,*
has the following paragraph on the influence of experimental and
meditative works : "One who imbues his mind with the spirit of
Augustine's *Confessions* finds no difficulty in understanding the
Song of Solomon.   An earthly exegesis can interpret this song
of songs only from its own point of view.   The conceptions, figures and terms of the spiritual lyric are instinctively referred to
earthly and carnal relationships.   An unspiritual mind cannot,
by any possibility, rise into the pure ether and element of incor-
poreal and heavenly beauty in which the writer of this canticle
moves his wings   But not so the Augustines, the Anselms and
the Bernards   These purged and clear eyes were granted at
certain favored hours, and as the result and reward of their long
vigils and meditations, the immortal vision of the pure in heart.
And the immortal vision wakened the immortal longing.   The
environment of earth and time became a prison to the now illu-

stone near him when he is mowing ;" the devout Christian is wise who has such a sanctified spiritual instrument within reach to put a finer edge upon his spirit

PRAYER : ITS TRANSFORMING INFLUENCE.

Special prominence should be given in these seasons of communion to prayer. Luke declares (ix. 28, 29) that Jesus, adhering to what appears to have been a habit, took the disciples at that time and " went up into a mountain to pray—" for the special purpose of prayer. Then behold the accompaniment of his prayer! "As he prayed, the fashion of his countenance was altered, and his raiment was white and glistering." As *he prayed!* And while earnest believing souls pray in spirit and in truth, a transforming influence is going on

minated spirit, and it pined for the hill of frankincense and the mountains of myrrh Having seen the King in his beauty, the holy and ethereal soul fell into love-longing " P. xxvi. Dr Shedd adds a note : " The experience of Edwards, as portrayed by himself, more than that of any other modern, exhibits these same characteristics. That rapt, exulting vision of the divine majesty and beauty which fell upon him like the dawn in the opening of his Christian life flushed his entire career, and entitles him also to the name of the 'angel c,' the 'seraphic' doctor."

in them. They are changed into the image of Christ from glory to glory as by the Spirit of God. The body, too, is influenced by it. Rapt communion with God! It at times bathes the face in a heavenly radiance and alters the fashion of the countenance. "All that sat in the council, looking steadfastly on Stephen, saw his face as it had been the face of an angel." Acts vi. 15. This effect of prayer should not be thought of as belonging exclusively to the revelation period of the past.

Krummacher, the author of *Elijah the Tishbite*, in his delightful *Autobiography* thus describes an intimate friend. " He was a mystic in the noblest sense of the word, and a man of prayer such as few then were. How often did the Lord seem near to him in most remarkable answers to prayers and in gracious help which he vouchsafed! Hence the peculiar gentle sunshine which seemed to irradiate his brow. Often when I looked upon him the words once written of Moses came to my remembrance: ' When he came down from the mount he knew not that the skin of his face shone when the Lord talked with him ' "

The soul chisels itself on the face Intense spiritual exercises will etherealize the countenance. Prayerful communion with God will make it shine with a heavenly lustre. And though the glorified Jesus be not present in the body, his spiritual presence is tenderly felt, and prepares for the hour when he shall be seen as he is.

> " Jesus, these eyes have never seen
> That radiant form of thine;
> The veil of sense hangs dark between
> Thy blessed face and mine.
>
> " I see thee not, I hear thee not,
> Yet art thou oft with me;
> And earth has ne'er so dear a spot
> As where I meet with thee.
>
> " Like some bright dream that comes unsought
> When slumbers o'er me roll,
> Thine image ever fills my thought,
> And charms my ravished soul.
>
> " Yet though I have not seen, and still
> Must rest in faith alone,
> I love thee, dearest Lord—and will,
> Unseen, but not unknown.
>
> " When death these mortal eyes shall seal,
> And still this throbbing heart,
> The rending veil shall thee reveal,
> All glorious as thou art "

DEVOTIONAL PIETY AND ACTIVITY.

4 A final lesson from this vision will guard against the abuse of the principle that has just been laid down. From our seasons of communion with heaven we must go back to the world and engage in its active and useful life.

When Peter saw the glory in which the person of his Lord was bathed, he answered and said to him, "Master, it is good for us to be here: and let us make three tabernacles, one for thee, and one for Moses, and one for Elias. For he wist not what to say: for he was sore afraid." But it was not his Lord's intention that they should tabernacle on that mount, and thereon enter for ever into that glory. They had no right to remain apart from their brethren and from their race of struggling men. A work remained for them to do. Sufferings were in store for them to endure. They must rejoin the other disciples and witness their Redeemer's death, and then go forth to many years' sacrifices and exertions for him

So, what is to be pleaded for from this example is not an ascetic life, which withdraws itself from the ordinary circles and affairs of the world. The

result of that has been evil, and only evil, continually. Self-contemplation and meditation and
devotional piety are not enough. These spiritual
exercises, refreshing and delightful as they are in
themselves, accomplish their greatest work only
as they enable us to live the better in the world,
be more holy in our intercourse with men, and
more effective in our labors for their salvation *
We cannot stay all the time in the mount of communion, away from our fellows. We must mingle
among them. We have duties to discharge in
reference to them. But if we will frequently go
apart by ourselves, and behold the King in his
glory, and have communion with him and with
the spirits of the just through their devotional
writings, grace and strength will be given us in

* One of Bacon's pregnant sentences is that with which, referring to an assertion in the *Politica* of Aristotle, he opens his
essay on *Friendship.* "It had been hard for him that spake it
to have put more truth and untruth together in few words than
in that speech, 'Whosoever is delighted in solitude is either a
wild beast or a god;' for it is most true that a natural and secret
hatred and aversion toward society in any man hath somewhat
of the savage beast; but it is most untrue that it should have
any character at all of the divine nature except it proceed, not
out of a pleasure in solitude, but *out of a love and desire to
sequester a man's self for a higher conversation.*"

large measure for our duties and trials on earth;
and every such season will be a foretaste of
heaven, and increase our longing for its eternal,
unbroken happiness.

FROM THE MOUNT TO THE WORLD.

From the mount of spiritual communion, then,
on the Sabbath in the sanctuary, and from your
closets, from the reading and the hearing of the
truth, and meditation upon it, and from prayerful
intercourse with your God, go out and go down
to the world to work for your Redeemer until he
comes to take you for ever to the glory whose
fringes only hang about you here. Be much in
thoughtful contact with God's truth and in prayer
to him, so that through those channels the stream
of life may flow as a mighty volume into your
souls; and out in the world bring that life into
full play; wrestle for your Redeemer; labor for
him; if need be, suffer manfully in imitation of
him. Everywhere and always have deeply sympathetic hearts for the weary mass of humanity
of which you form a part. Look on your race
as Jesus did. Take the food of this life, and the
richer bread of the life to come, to your fellows.
Go down to them, and endeavor to bring them up

to the height of the sacred mount, that they may
see the glory of Jesus. Strengthened by your
retired communion with the Lord from time to
time, seek out the suffering and the lost, and
strive to win them to heaven. If, with weak and
wearied body and anxious mind, the labor should
sometimes become very toilsome, and the heart
should grow despondent and long for perfect
rest, remember that soon the full and unintermitted glory shall come to you.

Jesus now wears in heaven the transfigured
form on which the three disciples gazed. Passing
through the grave, his body permanently assumed
the brightness which clothed it on the mount for
a little while. And those who are faithful to him
shall be like him and see him as he is; "For,"
cries out the most logical and yet the most emotional of the apostles, "our conversation is in
heaven, from whence also we look for the Saviour,
the Lord Jesus Christ, who shall change our vile
body, that it may be fashioned like unto his own
glorious body." Phil. iii. 20, 21.* Not only for an
hour, as upon the earthly mount, but throughout

* Strictly : "Who shall *transfigure* the body of our humiliation, that it may be conformed to the body of his glory." On
the mount he gave a sample of that coming transfiguration.

eternity, all the redeemed shall behold the bright transfiguration of their Lord, and be themselves transfigured ; and not only hear Moses and Elias talking with him, but themselves commune with them and with the great and the good of every age.

" Blessed who the King of heaven in his beauty thus behold,
  And beneath his throne rejoicing see a universe unfold,
  Sun and moon and stars and planets radiant in his light un-
      rolled "

IV.

*HEAVENLY RECOGNITION * THE SOCIAL LIFE.*

THE transfiguration of our Redeemer, as we have already seen, opened up to earth a temporary glimpse of the glory of heaven. Another of the facts which it very clearly exhibits is the social life of the celestial country. How strikingly the communion, the knowledge and the recognition of

* As this subject is one of such widespread and tender interest, and as some of my readers may desire to peruse some fuller exhibition of it, it may be well to mention an issue of the Presbyterian Board of Publication which I have glanced through while revising my manuscript—" *Our Friends in Heaven* By the Rev. J. M Killen " It is a small volume of 225 pages I think Mr. Killen, in his effort to weave a great many threads of evidence into his argument, claims for some passages of Scripture more than they contain ; and I am not sure but that, in his desire to meet unfounded objections, he is too anxious to get rid of the idea that " relative affections " have the " stamp of immortality impressed upon them " But the book is an exhaustive exhibition of the subject. Of course it is more minute on the special topic than a single section of a wider work can be.

the glorified redeemed are exemplified in it!
Moses and Elijah appear conversing with each
other and with Christ. We can scarcely suppose
that they issued out of a darkness which concealed them from each other in heaven, and, recognizing one another for the first time amid the
light on the mountain, returned to darkness again.
They did then on earth what they had often done
in the land of glory.

THE QUESTION AS TO HEAVENLY RECOGNITION

This, therefore, gives a point of departure for
the answer to a question that involves much of
our conception of the future, and has a very
practical bearing on the present life. Will those
who are Christian friends here know each other
in the glorious land, and there live anything like
the friendship-life of earth? Will they recognize
each other, and enjoy a social life similar to that
which is an important element of their happiness
in this stage of their existence?

Some doubt this. They have a vague idea
that every saved soul will be so much taken up
with Christ as neither to notice, nor even to wish
to notice, the other redeemed. I have met with
the story of a man whose pious wife had been

taken from him by death. He was asked whether
he supposed that when he reached heaven he
should recognize her. His reply was that, even
if it were possible to do it, he would be so
enraptured with the Lord Jesus that she might
be at his side for ages before he would think of
looking at her! *

* It was a more robust sanctified common sense which spake
in the rough retort of a Welshman to the question whether he
believed in recognition in heaven: "Do you think we shall be
greater fools there than here?" But the questioning on the subject, and the way in which it is referred to by writers, are
remarkable. The eloquent French Protestant Saurin, for
instance (in Sermon 55), alludes to it as "a famous question
in the schools," and asserts that "they who have taken the
affirmative side, and they who have taken the negative, have
often done so without any reason." He believes in the truth;
but the only consideration which he advances for it is that a
general judgment, righting the moral inequalities of this stage
of our existence, is a necessity, and that unless the saints should
know each other in the next life they could not acquiesce in the
justice of the sentence pronounced on all. And he thus illustrates that position: "Observe St. Paul, whose ministry was continually counteracted. What motive supported him under so
much opposition? Certainly it was the expectation of seeing
one day with his own eyes the conquest which he obtained for
Jesus Christ; souls which he had plucked out of the jaws of
Satan; believers whom he had guided to eternal happiness."
"And yet," says Knapp in his *Theology*, "there have been
Christians, and even teachers calling themselves *Christian*

11

To most Christians, however, such a view is very chilling. They wish to believe in, and do hope for, a mutual recognition in the better land. But perhaps comparatively few could give closely connected reasons for the hope that they indulge. I shall therefore present what strike me as the chief arguments in favor of the general truth, and shall so exhibit them as to give a somewhat definite view of the social life of the glorified, and invest them with a practical bearing on the present as a preparation for the future.

THR EXPECTATION OF BELIEVERS.

1. It is a strong presumption in favor of this truth that it is deeply seated in the enlightened consciousness of believers. The people of God live and die in the confident expectation of recognizing each other in heaven. The hope finds spontaneous expression in the utterances of the dying hour.

Recall one of the most touching incidents in the life of David. While his child was lying

teachers, who have blamed, and even ridiculed, other Christians for comforting themselves under the loss of those who were dear to them by cherishing the joyful hope of seeing them again and renewing after death the friendship here formed !"

sick he exhibited every token of distress, but
when it was reported to him that life had departed
from the little body, his whole demeanor changed,
so that his servants in surprise said, "What
thing is this that thou hast done? Thou didst
fast and weep for the child while it was alive, but
when the child was dead thou didst rise and eat
bread." 2 Sam. xii. 21. The answer of the afflicted king was a model one, expressive of anxious care and prayerful effort while there was the
slightest thread to hang upon, of resignation
when all earthly hope was gone, and of a de-
cided assurance of union in the world to come:
" While the child was alive I fasted and wept:
for I said, Who can tell whether God will be gracious to me, that the child may live? But now
he is dead, wherefore should I fast? Can I bring
him back again? I shall go to him; but he shall
not return to me."

"I shall go to him." Language more pertinent
could scarcely be found to indicate David's belief
that death was not an eternal separator, but that
when he too should die he should meet with his
child beyond the grave.

This record was written under the guidance of
the Holy Ghost; so that we have the assurance

that the incident actually occurred, and that it is
truthfully related to us.   But I do not press it as
the utterance of a special revelation which was
then made to David.   I quote it as an illustration
of what is the pervading religious belief and
feeling of God's people.   The grief of multitudes
of bereaved parents since has been transmuted
into a most glorious joy by the conviction of the
same truth.   They expected that when they
entered heaven their infants who had been taken
before them would spring to them as " springs a
sunbeam to the heart of flowers."

Not only do remaining Christians, at the summons of death, calmly give up their friends,
because they are sustained by the hope of a
reunion beyond the grave, but when they themselves are called upon to go down to the Jordan
of death, they do it in the assurance that those
whom they leave behind in Christ shall meet
with them again.   Doubtless, death has taken
away from many of my readers beloved friends
whose last words were, " Meet me in heaven."
The consolation which was ministered to them
was that the separation was not to be for ever.
Almost every Christian biography brings out
this point in bold relief.   At the failing hour of

earth's life, when, if ever, a false hope should break and error be banished from the mind, the Christian feels assured that the social life is not rudely snapt asunder, but that the complicated threads of sacred friendships are only dropped at death that they may be taken up and woven anew into a more glorious texture in the eternal life of heaven.

This must be the writing of God's Spirit upon the hearts of his people. A lesson in religious experience so general must have been learned of him. It is the utterance of a divinely-implanted hope.

RECOGNITION AMONG THE LOST.

2. An analogical argument is found in the fact that it is expressly asserted in the Bible that the lost recognize each other in the place of doom.

Isaiah, in the fourteenth chapter of his prophecy, portrays the destruction of Babylon and the overthrow of its king. In one of the boldest descriptions that has ever been attempted by poetry, after bringing before us the joy which this event caused through the earth, he changes the scene to *Hades*, whose inhabitants, especially the mighty ones that the king of Babylon had destroyed, he represents as recognizing and glorying

over the casting down of the oppressor: "Hell
from beneath is moved for thee to meet thee at
thy coming: it stirreth up the dead for thee, even
all the chief ones of the earth; it hath raised up
from their thrones all the kings of the nations.
All they shall speak and say unto thee, Art thou
also become weak as we? Art thou become like
unto us?" Isa. xiv. 9, 10. After death and beyond
the grave the wicked retain their power of recognizing those whom they knew on earth.

The parable of the rich man and Lazarus
(Luke xvi. 19–31) goes farther on this point.
The request that Abraham would send Lazarus
to the five brethren who still remained upon
the earth, that he might testify unto them, lest
they also should enter the place of torment,
assumes that the rich man knew that he would
recognize those brethren when they should arrive
in the lost world, and that for some reasons their
presence would add to his sufferings. It was
from no love to them that he wanted them kept
away.* The most likely supposition is that he

* "There is here no waking up of good in the heart of the
lost, but, as Trench acutely remarks, bitter reproach against God
and the old economy as not having warned him sufficiently.
Abraham's answer rolls back the reproach with calm dignity as

had been the instrument in leading them astray while he was with them; and he knew that the sight of them tossing upon the waves of suffering would give his conscience a more scorpion sting when he should remember that but for him they might have been saved.

In this parable our Lord further indicates a knowledge by the lost of the happiness of the saved, and a knowledge by the saved of the misery of the lost The rich man, lifting up his eyes toward the abode of the blessed, saw Abraham, and with him Lazarus, whom he had known and despised while upon earth, while they also beheld the misery of the condemned soul.   What a recognition was that of those who had known each other in this life!

If it be said that this is the mere drapery of a parable, and that it is not to be pressed for the support of such a startling assertion, I reply that the same truth is more fearfully presented by the great Teacher in one of his simple didactic statements: "There shall be weeping and gnashing of teeth when ye shall *see* Abraham and Isaac and Jacob, and all the prophets " (and among them

unmerited: 'They are sufficiently warned.' "—*Brown* on Luke xvi. 28.

John the Baptist, whom they had seen and known in the flesh), "in the kingdom of God, and you yourselves thrust out." Luke xiii. 28.

Now, if the make of human nature be such that those who go to perdition carry with them through the grave the power of recognition to their confusion and pain, we cannot suppose for a moment that those who enter heaven will not retain the same power to their everlasting enjoyment.

THE DESCRIPTIONS OF LAST THINGS.

3. The descriptions which the Bible gives of "the last things" involve this truth, and throw light on the practical nature of it and on its connection with our conduct here. Men appear in them all not merely as individuals, but as social beings, recognizing and communing with each other.

Most clearly does this appear in the representations of the judgment. That is to be a judicial transaction. Not merely is the eternal destiny of all men to be declared, but in the presence of each other and of the assembled universe an impartial trial is to be had, and the sentence of each is to be publicly awarded upon evidence,

so that God's ways may be vindicated to all. Not
only are the books to be opened—the book of God's
providential dealings with each person ; the books
of memory and conscience, accusing or justifying ;
and the book of life, declaring whether the name
has been registered therein from eternity—but
men are to be witnesses for and against each other.
Those who have here met, and in their daily
conduct influenced each other, shall stand before
the Judge and give their mutual evidence.*

* Difficulties, suggested by our present clumsy physical being,
may very easily be raised about this. "The older theologians
speculated on the manner in which the judgment is to be
arranged, so as to admit of the countless millions of human
beings who shall have lived from the beginning of the world
to the final consummation being so congregated as to be all
gathered before the throne of the Son of man The common
answer to that difficulty was, that the throne is to be so exalted
and so glorious as to be visible, as are the sun and moon, from
a large part of the earth's surface at the same time. . . . How
far the descriptions of the process of the last judgment given in
the Bible are to be understood literally it is useless to inquire.
Two things are remarkable about the prophecies of Scripture
which have already been accomplished. The one is, that the
fulfillment has, in many cases, been very different from that
which a literal interpretation led men to anticipate. The other
is, that in some cases they have been fulfilled even to the most
minute details. These facts should render us modest in our interpretation of those predictions which remain to be accomplished,

Turn to the dramatic representation of this transaction by the Saviour, Matt. xxv. 31–46. Listen to the award. "Come," the Judge says to the righteous—"Come, ye blessed of my Father, inherit the kingdom prepared for you from the foundation of the world." Then notice the enumeration of the acts of kindness which they had done to him. In surprise they say, "When saw we thee ahungered and fed thee, or thirsty and gave thee drink? When saw we thee a stranger and took thee in, or naked and clothed thee? Or when saw we thee sick or in prison, and came unto thee?" Behold him turning to others whom they had benefited and saying, "Inasmuch as ye have done it unto one of the least of these my brethren, ye have done it unto me." There they stand, in the presence of each other and of the Judge, fully recognizing each other as those who had performed and received acts of kindness for Christ's sake. That one description embalms

satisfied that what we know not now we shall know hereafter." Dr. Hodge's *Theology,* iii. 849, 850 Bickersteth poetically pictures the judgment throne:

> "In heaven, immediately above
> The holy hills of Zion as it seemed,
> Though peradventure airy semblance veil'd
> A distance greater than the solar orb"

some of the most tender friendships of earth for the memories of heaven. We shall recognize those to whom we do acts of kindness here, and the recollection of those acts will draw the greater happiness from their society.

This gives point to such an exhortation as that which Paul addressed to the Philippians (ch. ii. 14–16): "Do all things without murmurings and disputings, that ye may be blameless and harmless, the sons of God without rebuke in the midst of a crooked and perverse generation, among whom ye shine as lights in the world, holding forth the word of life, that I may rejoice in the day of Christ that I have not run in vain, neither labored in vain." That is: So live, so persevere in the holy following of Christ, that in the judgment day I may behold you on his right hand, and rejoice with you in seeing that my labors have been blessed to your eternal salvation. It would fritter away the beauty and the force of this passage to say that the apostle could rejoice in having the knowledge communicated to him by God that those Philippians were saved. They are to stand together in the presence of the Lord —they around the apostle as his crown of rejoicing.

It is but extending the principle of the passage to say that not merely shall the pastor rejoice in beholding the public reception into heaven of those who have been through him led to the Saviour, but that every Christian who in the daily walks of life has been importunate in prayer, and spoken for Jesus, and commended religion by a consistent example, and thus guided a soul to the Saviour, shall rejoice in meeting that friend beyond the grave and in having an everlasting fellowship with him.

Those whom we lead or by whom we are led to Jesus—

> "In the world to come, should they go first,
> How warm will be their greeting, when, with toils
> Finished on earth, we reach Jerusalem
> Which is above, and these in glory see
> Where the saints dwell and Christ for ever reigns!
> Be this our consolation and our hope."

This, I suppose, will be one principle on which the associations of heaven will be formed. There will be a special bond of union through eternity between the Christian who was instrumental in leading others to the Saviour and those whom he thus influenced. Oh the happiness of hearing from saved souls the declaration—

" From thy mouth we heard of Jesus' love,
And thine the hand that led us to his feet !' "

The various forms under which heaven and its happiness are presented in the Bible most beautifully embody the truth that I am presenting.

When the glorified redeemed are spoken of as the family of God in heaven, does it not suggest the knowledge and communion of its various members, in which

" Every loving heart
Shall reflect joy to joy, and light to light
Like crystals in a cave flashing with fire,
And multiply their bliss a million-fold " ?

When all are represented as singing the same song, and making heaven vocal with their melody, can we for an instant suppose that they shall for ever remain unacquainted with each other ? As isolated beings, beholding only Christ himself, are they to be singing that song ? Can we imagine a congregation uniting in the worship of God here, Sabbath after Sabbath, and all its various members remaining ignorant of each other ? Does not the expression imply communion ? Can there be communion without mutual knowledge and love ? And can we suppose that there will be knowledge, recognition, communion among those who were personally strangers here, and that the Christian fellowships of this life shall be banished? Will we, if we enter heaven, form new and eternal friendships with some whom we never heard of here, and shall we never even happen to meet with each other? Can we suppose that God will act so contrary to our nature as deliberately to keep us apart, never permit us to meet, or if we should meet that there would be no recognition and special love? The Christian fellowships of this life broken off, and only new ones to be formed? Ah no! The happiness of reunion after a temporary separation shall be one element in heaven's joy to the redeemed soul as it enters the blessed land. What a Christian poet * has pictured, in vision, of his soul after death is, I doubt not, daily realized:

> " I was no stranger in a strange land there;
>   But rather as one who, travel-worn and weary—
>   Weary of wandering through many climes—
>   At length returning homeward, eyes far off
>   The white cliffs of his fatherland, and ere
>   The laboring ship touches its sacred soil
>   Leaps on the pier, while round him crowding press
>   Children, and kith, and friends, who in a breath

* Bickersteth in *Yesterday, To-day and For Ever.*

Ask of his welfare, and with joyous tongues
Pour all their love into his thirsty ear.
Such welcome home was mine, such questionings
Of things that had befallen me since last
We met, and of my pathway thitherward,
And of the dear ones I had left behind—
Words with embraces interspersed. . . .
　　　　　Every step
Some fondly-loved, familiar face was seen
Whom I had known in pilgrim days, unchanged,
And yet all bright with one similitude :
One Lord had looked on them."

How tenderly suggestive of the home-life of the blessed place are the mansions which Christ says he prepares for his people! There is an infinite number of abodes in the better land, in which the saved live, not separately, one individual in each mansion, secluded from all the rest, but grouped together according to some laws of association, the same in principle, doubtless, as those which bind together kindred spirits on earth. "Heaven is furnished with every accommodation. In it all those comforts will be found which we usually enjoy in a house—rest, peace, society, and friendship. It is the place of final meeting to the children of God, as the members of a human family who are separated during the day, and scattered abroad in pursuit of their respective

employments, assemble in the evening in their
common habitation."   From the public and
enrapturing service of song which rolls up to the
eternal throne, and from the varied employments
for the glory of the Most High in which they
will be engaged, the saved shall have their smaller
circles of associates to whom they can return, and
with whom, in the mansions provided for them,
they will have special fellowship.   And I fear not
to say that they will often retire to those abodes
with something like the thrilling song, "There's
no place like home."   Within the one glorious
home there will be special homes for souls of
special congeniality,

"Where each may be alone with God,
Or mix in converse with his fellow-saints at will."

If I should be privileged to reach the blessed
place, I doubt not that

"Oft in my mansion will some elder saint
Linger and tell his story or ask mine,
Or I will listen from an infant's lips
A tale of such delightsomeness as pours
New meaning into words henceforth.   And oft
A group of the beatified, enlinked
In all the bonds of holy lineage,
Will cluster underneath the trees of life,

One eye kindling another, one deep thought
Waking another thought, and this another,
Until all bosoms overflow with love;
And all perforce will hasten to the throne,
And at their Father's footstool pour their hearts
In one full tide of common rapture forth."

HUMAN NATURE IN HEAVEN THE SAME AS HERE.

4. A further fact which both proves and explains the truth that I am exhibiting is, that the redeemed enter heaven with precisely the same nature that they had here—purified and exalted indeed, but not essentially changed. Its powers and capacities are strengthened; none of them is lost. The kingdom of heaven in glory is the continuation, the extension, the perfection of the kingdom of heaven which is set up in the hearts that are regenerated here by the Spirit of God. Death does not disrupt the soul and leave a portion of it behind, nor does it destroy any of our spiritual capabilities or acquisitions. It passes the soul into the presence of God free from sin, and from all the effects of sin, which show themselves in contracting our powers, limiting our knowledge, cramping our affections and weakening our activities

The inhabitants of heaven do not cease to love;

12

and to love they must know, recognize, mingle among, commune and work with each other.

Their knowledge is not less than it was here; it is vastly increased.

Their memory does not cease to act. It retains the treasures which it has accumulated through the life of earth, and especially its recollections of God's dealings with them, of their connection with each other and of their common labors for him. That alone would make certain the recognition and special association in heaven of those who have been associated in Christian bonds on earth Deeply written upon their memories shall be their sanctified friendships. Therefore, if after friends have been separated for years which have left their changing impress upon the body, so that the external form scarcely remains the same, they will yet recognize each other by a tone of the voice, or a quick lighting up of the face with an old familiar smile, or by some mental characteristic, and then together live over the days of their childhood and recount to each other the scenes through which they have passed, much more may we rest assured that in the glorious light of heaven reunited friends shall quickly know of the presence of each other, and with joy com-

mune about what God the Lord has done for
them;

> " And what delights can equal those
>   That stir the spirit's inner deeps
>   When one that loves, but knows not, reaps
>   A truth from one that loves and knows ?"

The ear will detect the footstep of a beloved
one before he is in sight, or be at once attracted
by his voice in a choir of singers; amid the perfectly refined spiritualities of heaven soul will
answer to soul, and quickly clasp each other in
the bonds of eternal love.*

* A friend was speaking to me recently of the difficulty which
she had in conceiving how those who are here separated by
death could find each other and have a special mutual recognition in such an immense place as heaven is, and among the
innumerable multitude that are there. Separated by death for
years, and perhaps far apart locally, how can they be certain of
thus coming together ? But God who calleth the innumerable
stars by name can be trusted for that. Baxter has a simile (in
ch. iii. of his *Dying Thoughts*) which expresses more than lies
upon its surface, and has an application here· "Nor need we
wonder how a whole world of glorified bodies can all of them
be present with the one body of Christ; for as solar beams are
so present with the air that none can discern the difference of
the places which they possess, and a world of bodies are present
with them both, so may all our bodies, without any confusion,
be present with Christ's body."

EVERY SOURCE OF SPIRITUAL JOY CONTINUES.

5. A final argument on the question is, that every source of spiritual happiness that is possessed here by the saved continues in heaven.

There are no sinful enjoyments there. Pleasures which arise from the present constitution of our bodies are left in the grave. They shall not find a place in the glorified forms that shall arise at the last day. But we have no reason to suppose that any pure spring of happiness from which the soul now drinks shall ever cease its enlivening stream.

Now, one of the purest, most refined and refining pleasures which we possess is that which flows from the friendship and communion of Christian souls. If the kingdom of glory is anything like the kingdom of grace, if the joys which the Spirit bestows here are foretastes of the joys of the heavenly country, there is no such thing as isolation there. Forming new friendships, those who specially knew and loved each other on earth shall ever be bound together by the recollection of their earthly life. The infinite range of heaven's companionships shall never cause them to forget the contracted circle of earth's attachments.

This is not inconsistent with that perfect and concentrated love which is bestowed upon the divine Redeemer. As surely as we love him, we love all the brethren, while we bestow a special love on those who are nearest to us. And surely if, in hearts that are still under the influence of sin, the two may coexist, each strengthening the other, the holiness of heaven is accompanied by the perfection of both.

Jesus in his life upon earth gave us a view of the life of heaven. "With supreme love to God, he loved his Church, and gave himself for it; with love to his Church, he loved the disciples as his own; while again within this circle one of them was specially *the* loved one; and beyond it he loved Martha and Mary and Lazarus." There can scarcely be any presumption in supposing that in glory he still retains a special love for that little family of Bethany under whose roof he was so often sheltered, and in regard to one of whom, when affliction had entered the house, the other members were warranted in sending the simple message, "He whom thou lovest is sick." John xi. 3.

Let it not be doubted that there are in heaven special circles of friends, determined by peculiar

16

sinless temperaments, by habits formed here, and by works prosecuted for the Lord.

The renewal of old and earth-consecrated friendships will not prevent the formation of new and more widely extended ones. There are impediments in the way of having many deep attachments in this world. Friendships are bounded and restrained. In heaven the impediments are doubtless removed; and while we will specially associate with those friends in Christ to whom we were particularly attached here, we suppose we shall also recognize and enjoy communion with many whom we never met on earth. Through their history or through their writings we become acquainted with persons upon whom we never lay our eyes, and soul becomes united to soul. In heaven, to use an expression of Luther, as Adam immediately recognized Eve when she was brought to him, we may recognize those pure spirits of inspired and uninspired sacred history with whom we have often and deeply communed through their biographies.*

---

* " We shall see them, the magnates of God's kingdom, the sacred ideals of our minds, the beloved of our hearts. It will be an ever-new meeting and recognition."—Luthardt's *Saving Truths of Christianity*, p. 271.

Another series of joyful recognitions heaven also witnesses day by day. Most loving friends we have who know us intimately, though we are not yet acquainted with them personally. " How often does it happen to us in regard to our earthly friends that those who are unknown to us in our early years even by name become in our later years indissolubly bound up with our history and our joy! And thus the angels, whom on earth we have never seen, will nevertheless become our intimate friends and dear companions for ever. Let us not forget, however, that the angels know each saint on earth more intimately than the saints themselves are known by their nearest friends. For ' are they not all ministering spirits, sent forth to minister for them who shall be heirs of salvation ?' But this fact suggests another analogy between our social relationships with men and angels—viz., that as earthly friends who have been acquainted with ourselves and our family history during the forgotten days of infancy are met by us, in after years, not as strangers, but with feelings of sympathy and intimacy akin to those awakened by old kindred, even so will the saint, on reaching heaven, find God's angels to be not strangers, but old friends who have known all about him from the day of his birth until the hour of his death." *

How delightful this sociability! After we enter their home, to recognize and commune with those who, as divinely-appointed guardians, have watched over and ministered to us through our earthly course, and who shall at death escort our souls in triumph through the pearly gate! How blissful to become personally acquainted with those who have known us from the first, and who can tell us so much in explanation of the past, and introduce us to so much of the future! How rich their knowledge gathered through the ages! how tender their sympathy! how helpful their guidance!

Our angel friends—unknown *to* us now, but revealed in person in heaven—peculiar friendly circles they will form for us in the glorious land.

RECOGNITION NOT POSTPONED UNTIL THE RESUR- RECTION.

The transfiguration scene shows that the heavenly recognition is not postponed until the resur-

* Dr. Norman McLeod's *Parish Papers,* 123

rection. The body of Elijah, it is true, had been translated, and he probably wore it at that eventful interview; but that of Moses was buried and had not yet risen. So that, whatever objections might be suggested by the difficulty of recognizing the glorified body because of the different form which it shall wear (though, if we take the body of Jesus after his resurrection as that which our bodies are to be like, the difficulties would not seem to arise; for the disciples recognized him *), they really do not bear upon the subject.

* But the following, from Westcott's *Gospel of the Resurrection* (third English edition, p. 162), is suggestive: "This body, which was recognized as essentially the same body, had yet undergone some marvelous change, of which we can gain a faint idea by what is directly recorded of its manifestations. (It is not, I believe, a mere fancy to see a typical indication of this change in the words used by our Lord himself of his glorified body. Luke xxiv. 39; comp. Eph v. 30. The significant variation from the common formula, 'flesh and blood,' must have been at once intelligible to Jews accustomed to the provisions of the Mosaic ritual, and nothing would have impressed upon them more forcibly the transfiguration of Christ's body than the verbal omission of the element of blood, which was for them the symbol and seat of corruptible life.) Thus we find that the person of Christ was not recognized directly by those who saw him. However firm their conviction was afterward that they had 'seen the Lord,' they knew him first when he was pleased to make himself known. Human sense alone was not capable of

There is a spiritual recognition which we have
here in some degree, and which perfectly exists
in the eternal world. The soul is active between
death and the resurrection; this communion of
departed spirits goes on now in the upper sanctuary; and even the eyes of the three disciples
were miraculously touched and enabled to get a
glimpse of it. Our redeemed friends who have
already been taken home are waiting to see our
souls borne to heaven by attending angels, and

discerning who he was. It could not be otherwise if his body
was glorified, for our senses can only apprehend that which is of
kindred nature with themselves. At one time (Matt. xxviii 9;
John xx. 16, 19) it was by a word of personal or general tenderness, that Christ awakened the faith by which sense was
quickened; at another time (Luke xxiv. 30, 31) by the celebra-
tion of that holy rite which he had instituted before his death;
at another (John xxi.) by a mighty act which symbolized the
blessing of the apostolic work. And as Christ's body was no
longer necessarily to be recognized, so also was it not bound by
the material laws to which its action was generally conformed.
He is found present, no one knows from whence He passes
away, no one knows whither. He stands in the midst of the
little group of the apostles 'when the doors were shut, for fear of
the Jews.' John xx. 'He vanished out of sight' (Luke xx. 31)
of those whose eyes were opened that they knew him. And at
last, 'while they beheld, he was taken up, and a cloud received
him out of their sight.' Acts i 9 "

to seek a renewal of sacred communion with us.*

For the reasons which have thus been given, I feel sure not only that heaven is a social place, and that its inhabitants enjoy a most holy and happy communion with each other while they are engaged in the worship of God and in studying his works and working for him, but that the sanctified friendships of this life are perpetuated, extended, and freed from the defilements of sin and the limitations of the mortal body; and that while all who have been intimately associated in Christ will continue, in a far higher degree, their earthly communion, they shall also enjoy the fellowship of the great and the good of all ages and of all climes.

The proof is cumulative. Each argument is sufficient to establish the position. The chain, drawn as it is from the word of God and appeal-

* Knapp, after referring to the heathen ideas on this subject, says very pithily, "The soul, indeed, is no longer regarded as a fine material substance, as it often was in ancient times; but these delightful views lose nothing on this account, as some have most unphilosophically supposed. For one may be recognized otherwise than by his body, and may be loved, too, otherwise than corporeally. Why, then, should not departed souls recognize each other, even when they no longer possess bodies?"

ing to the spiritually enlightened consciousness,
places it beyond doubt. To recapitulate: It is a
presumptive argument that believers almost uni-
versally anticipate this reunion and friendship.
The presumption is strengthened by the fact that
it is clearly stated that there is recognition among
the lost. The Bible descriptions of the second
coming of Christ, the resurrection, the judgment
and heaven involve it. The redeemed inhabitants
of earth take to the other world precisely the
nature which they have here, though freed from
sin and imperfection, with all its powers and treas-
ured recollections. And every pure source of
spiritual happiness which they enjoy in this world
is continued in heaven.

PRACTICAL TEACHINGS.

Very powerful are the practical lessons for this
life which are involved in this great and far-reaching truth.

COMFORTING FOR MOURNERS.

1. It is peculiarly comforting in the hours of
earthly bereavement.

Our friends whom the Lord by his death-angel
calls away are not lost to us in any sense; nor

when we shall be taken shall we be lost to those
whom we leave behind. There is a temporary
suspension of communion, but on neither side is
there forgetfulness, and the hour of unbroken
reunion cometh. Let us cultivate the habit of
anticipating it as the eternal restoration, in a perfect spirituality, of the communion of earth. Our
departed ones are at rest with the Beloved, in the
unalloyed enjoyment of communion with other
members of the General Assembly and Church
of the first-born, with the spirits of just men
made perfect, with the innumerable company of
angels, and with Jesus the Mediator of the new
covenant.

> " They do not die,
> Nor lose their mortal sympathy,
> Nor change to us, although they change."

Their happiness is perfect, though not complete
—not complete, because they wait for us, and for
the glorious appearing of the Lord, when they
shall come with him to reclaim their bodies; for
"if we believe that Jesus died and rose again,
even so them also which sleep in Jesus will God
bring with him." I Thess. iv. 14. Be it ours, then,
not to sorrow as those who have no hope, nor
unceasingly to mourn the departure of the beloved

who have fallen asleep in Jesus, but rather to rejoice that they are free from all trouble, and to be ready to obey the summons of the Lord when he comes to us, so that we may meet them again.

> " A few more years shall roll,
>   A few more seasons come,
>   And we shall be with those that rest
>   Asleep within the tomb.
>
> " A few more struggles here,
>   A few more partings o'er,
>   A few more toils, a few more cares,
>   And we shall weep no more."

EXALTS LIFE'S SANCTIFIED FRIENDSHIPS.

2. This truth gives an infinite value to the sanctified friendships of this life. They are not among the perishable relations of earth, and therefore they are to be the more highly esteemed.

Mere physical and blood connections do pass away. In the heavenly world "they neither marry nor are given in marriage." Matt. xxii. 30. "There will be no wedlock, no sexual propensities, and no gross material bodies therein. Friendship in virtuous and pious minds, however, does not depend upon these circumstances, but rather upon intellectual tastes and dispositions. What, therefore, is merely sensual and corporeal in love and friendship here will there fall away; but whatever is spiritual, which is the essential and nobler part of friendship, will remain and constitute a great part of the bliss of heaven." This most certainly does not involve the cessation of a peculiar affection between those who have been related on earth. One can sympathize with Charles Kingsley's vigorous protest against the monkish perversion of our Lord's teaching: " All I can say is, if I do not love my wife, body and soul, as well there as I do here, then there is neither resurrection of my body nor of my soul, but of some other, and I shall not be I." " I know that if immortality is to include, in my case, identity of person, I shall feel to her for ever what I feel now. That feeling may be developed in ways which I do not expect; it may have provided for it forms of expression very different from any which are among the holiest sacraments of life; of that I take no care. The union I believe to be as eternal as my own soul." "And how are the angels of God in heaven? Is there no love among them? If the law which makes two beings unite themselves, and crave to unite

themselves, in body, soul and spirit, be the law of
earth—of pure humanity—if, so far from being
established by the Fall, this law has been the one
from which the Fall has made mankind deflect
most in every possible way; if the restoration of
purity and the restoration of this law are synony-
mous; if love be of the Spirit—the vastest and
simplest exercise of will of which we can conceive,—then why should not this law hold in the
spiritual world as well as in the natural? In
heaven they neither marry nor are given in
marriage; but is not marriage the mere approxi-
mation to a unity which shall be perfect in
heaven? What if many have been alone on
earth? May they not find their kindred spirit in
heaven, and be united to it by a tie still deeper
than marriage? And shall we not be reunited in
heaven by that still deeper tie? Surely on earth
God has loved, Christ the Lord has loved, some
more than others: why should not we do the
same in heaven, and yet love all? Here the
natural body can but strive to express its love,
its desire of union. Will not one of the proper-
ties of the spiritual body be, that it will be able
to express that which the natural body only tries
to express?" "Does not the course of nature

point to this? What else is the meaning of the gradual increase of love on earth? What else is the meaning of old age, when the bodily powers die while the love increases? What does that point to but to a restoration of the body when mortality is swallowed up of life? Is not that mortality of the body sent us mercifully by God, to teach us that our love is spiritual, and therefore will be able to express itself in any state of existence?—to wean our hearts, that we may look for more perfect bliss in the perfect body? . . . Do not these thoughts take away from all earthly bliss the poisoning thought, 'All this must end?' Ay, end! but only end so gradually that we shall not miss it, and the less perfect union on earth shall be replaced in heaven by perfect and spiritual bliss and union, inconceivable because perfect! Do I undervalue earthly bliss? No! I enhance it when I make it the sacrament of a higher union. Will not these thoughts give more exquisite delight, will it not tear off the thorn from every rose and sweeten every nectar-cup to perfect security of blessedness in this life, to feel that there is more in store for us—that all expressions of love here are but dim shadows of a union which shall be perfect if we will but work here

so as to work out our salvation?"* In this
there is a very precious truth.

Though the earthly duties and promptings
connected with fleshly relationships shall cease,
they will be remembered, and, sanctified by grace,
will be attended with a sweeter enjoyment than
we have ever had here. The friendships which
will last are those which come through Jesus.
We should therefore be careful in forming them.
The followers of Christ should be our most
intimate friends.

> " True bliss, if man may reach it, is composed
>   Of hearts in union mutually disclosed;
>   And, farewell else all hope of pure delight,
>   Those hearts should be reclaimed, renewed, upright."

We should be very tender in preserving them.
Those who are to dwell together as friends in
heaven should be very forbearing with each other
in the region of sin. We should endeavor to
make the life of heaven our life on earth. We
should put down the unkind thought, the harsh
word, the unfriendly act, by remembering that if

* Charles Kingsley: *His Letters and Memoirs of his Life*
(American edition), pp. 267, 299-302.

we indulge them we soil that which is to be a part of our heritage for ever And we should the more strongly love the bond that unites us here because it is to last through eternity.

" I must confess," says Baxter, " as the experience of my own soul, that the expectation of loving my friends in heaven principally kindles my love to them while on earth. If I thought I should never know, and consequently never love them after this life, I should number them with temporal things, and love them as such; but I now delightfully converse with my pious friends in a firm persuasion that I shall converse with them for ever; and I take comfort in those that are dead or absent, believing that I shall shortly meet them in heaven and love them with a heavenly love."

Let us keep in loving communion with those who have been called from earth, though in person and in space we are separated for a time from each other. Let this have a holy influence upon us day by day ; for

> " How pure at heart and sound in head,
>   With what divine affections bold,
>   Should be the man whose thought would hold
>   An hour's communion with the dead !

" In vain shalt thou, or any, call
    The spirits from their golden day,
    Except, like them, thou too canst say,
My spirit is at peace with all.

" They haunt the silence of the breast,
    Imaginations calm and fair,
    The memory like a cloudless air,
The conscience as a sea at rest.

" But when the heart is full of din,
    And doubt beside the portal waits,
    They can but listen at the gates
And hear the household jar within."

PLEA FOR BENEVOLENT ACTS.

3. On this truth is founded a strong plea for the exercise of friendly and benevolent acts.

" Make to yourselves," says our Lord in Luke xvi. 9, "friends of the mammon of unrighteousness; that when ye fail they may receive you into everlasting habitations."* Offices of kindness toward disciples in the name of Christ secure for you those who will on the battlements of heaven wait your entrance, that they may usher you into the presence of their Redeemer with the sweetest of converse and with the decla-.

* That is: " Make to yourselves friends by the use of riches, that when you die the friends thus made may receive you into everlasting mansions."

ration of what you have done for them. Or if you should be taken home first, they will seek you out amid the shining throng of the ransomed, and intensify your eternal happiness. It is worth while to use the means which God has given us in doing good for the sake of the good itself: it will also add to the bliss of heaven, because as the redeemed shall always be praising the Redeemer for the great gift which he brought to them as lost sinners, so those whom we may benefit will never cease to tell of our kindness and love. Weary not, then, in doing good in your homes, your neighborhood, your church and the world, in any way in which the opportunity is presented. Whatever share of the riches of the world the Master has bestowed upon you, with it thus make friends who may welcome you to your everlasting mansion and add to your joy therein.

EARNEST LABORS FOR SALVATION OF FRIENDS.

4. Still stronger is the plea which should be drawn from this truth for earnestness in efforts for the salvation of friends.

A great stumbling-block in the way of the unhesitating reception of it is the idea (it has been advanced to me in conversation by most earnest-minded Christians who have beloved ones among the unconverted) that if friends recognize each other as among the saved in heaven, they must miss those who are not in the number, and that would cause them pain.

Probably, if anything could lead a true believer in God to reject a clear intimation of his word, it would be such an objection if no sufficient answer could be given to it. But even for a humanly unanswerable objection such as this we dare not deny a divine truth.

I barely suggest that in heaven the subjection to the will of God will be complete, and that if, after the repeated offers of his mercy, the Son of God can cast from his presence those who have rejected him, if He who wept over the coming destruction of Jerusalem and the horrible woes of its inhabitants strikes with the sword of his wrath, a way of escape will be provided by which the most tender-hearted of his people shall not have the happiness of heaven marred by this knowledge.*

* Saurin, in his very brief and passing reference to this question of recognition (and in the wide range of his splendid sermons he only thus touches upon it), compactly sums up the

But, believers in Jesus, be influenced by this truth to be unintermitted and unceasing in your efforts to bring your impenitent friends to him. For their deliverance from eternal wrath, for the increase of your own happiness, for the glory of

opposing arguments, and in that throws out an important truth bearing on the point which I make above:

" On the one side, the first " (the Scholastics who argued for recognition) " have pretended to establish their thesis on this principle that something would be wanting to our happiness if we were not to know in a future state those persons with whom we had been united by tenderest connections in this present world. On the other hand, if we know, say the partisans of the opposite opinion, the condition of our friends in a future state, how will it be possible that a parent should be happy in the possession of a heaven in which his children have no share? and how can he possibly relish pleasure at the right hand of God while he revolves this dreadful thought in his mind, My children are now, and will for ever be, tormented with the devil? It should seem the proof and the objection are equally groundless. The enjoyment of God is so sufficient to satiate a soul that it cannot be considered as necessary to the happiness of it to renew such connections as were formed during a momentary passage through this world. I oppose this against the argument for the first opinion. And I oppose the same against the objection; for the enjoyment of God is every way so sufficient to satiate a soul that it can love nothing but in God, and that its felicity cannot be altered by the miseries of those with whom there will then be no connection."

your Redeemer, spare no pains to accomplish this great result. By your consistent example commend the gospel to them. By your tender and faithful conversation point them to Jesus. By your importunate prayers bring down the grace of God upon them, so that they and you may shine as the stars for ever and ever. Labor on, pray on, hope on, even though you see no immediate result. The seed which you plant may yet spring up. The Spirit of God may take it at the last moment and cause it to be the means of leading the soul to salvation.

WARNING TO THE IMPENITENT.

5. A word of warning is not out of place here, though I am exhibiting heaven and its friendships. The darkest descriptions of the world of woe which are to be found in the Bible fell from the lips of the loving Jesus. He uttered them that with tones of love he might warn his hearers against the dread reality. Let it be observed, then, that in any who lead others astray and are the means of casting them down to eternal ruin, either by example or by words, the knowledge of their victims' misery will add a hundred-fold to the bitterness of their own suffering. The rich

man of the parable dreaded this; so may the skeptic, the immoral man, the false professor still. Again, if any continue and die impenitent while others around them press into the kingdom of God, it will increase their pain to remember that they might have been as happy as the others. Therefore, while the door of heaven is open, and the great Friend of humanity stands beckoning to all to enter, join the living stream of those who, loving him and loving each other, are pressing toward the delightful communion of his everlasting mansions.

V.

OUT OF GREAT TRIBULATION: THE SUFFERING LIFE.

TO be constantly in the enjoyment of health, so that in the pursuit of business and pleasure we may run and not be weary, and walk and not faint; to have the family circle unbroken, and never to be compelled to wear the weeds of mourning; to have business go on prosperously, and bring into our coffers a continued stream of wealth; never to have the voice of detraction lifted up against us, but to have all men speak well of us; to have our life like one perpetual May day, when the zephyrs gently blow and the earth wears her most beautiful appearance of green, when the lightnings flash not and the thunders roar not, when Nature dies not, but all things are full of promise and bursting with joyful anticipation; to be sheltered from

202

every blast, and never to have the simoom of sorrow rudely blow across us,—this, the world declares, would be perfect happiness; this all undis-
ciplined hearts would desire to have; and when
the Lord has been pleased to cause the waters of
affliction to roll over them, in the bitterness of
their spirits men are strongly tempted to curse
the day in which they were born, and to say, as
Naomi said to her old acquaintances, "Call me
not Naomi [that is, pleasant], call me Mara [that
is, bitter]; for the Almighty hath dealt very bit-
terly with me. I went out full, and the Lord hath
brought me home again empty; why then call
ye me Naomi, seeing the Lord hath testified
against me, and the Almighty hath afflicted
me?" Ruth i. 20, 21.

But God in his word and believers in their
thoughtful experience declare that though afflictions are the fruits of sin in the world, yet in this
fallen state they are so subsidized by the providence and grace of God as to promote our usefulness and happiness here, and hereafter to lead to
bliss in its perfection.

In Old Testament times God thus addressed
his people by Isaiah (xlviii. 10): "Behold, I have
refined thee, but not with silver; I have chosen

thee in the furnace of affliction." By various
calamities he had refined them as metal in a
furnace; and though they were not fully purified, as refined silver, but still had a great mixture
of base metal among them, yet he would again
choose them amidst the afflictions of Babylon, as
he had their fathers in the iron furnace of Egypt.

One of the apocalyptic visions (Rev. vii. 9–17)
also reveals, in a grand and enrapturing form, the
purifying influence of tribulation under the grace
of God, and the wonderfully contrasted happiness
to which sanctified sorrows lead.

"WHAT ARE THESE?"

The seer beheld (vs. 9, 10), "a great multitude
which no man could number, of all nations, and
kindreds, and people, and tongues," who "stood
before the throne, and before the Lamb, clothed
with white robes, and palms in their hands, and
cried with a loud voice, saying, Salvation to our
God which sitteth upon the throne, and unto the
Lamb!"

"What are these which are arrayed in white
robes?" asked one of the elders, "and whence
came they?"

His own reply (vs. 14–17), in words than

which none sweeter, more musical, more thrilling in the hearts of the great masses of Christ's followers can be found, was:

" These are they which came out of great tribulation, and have washed their robes, and made them white in the blood of the Lamb. Therefore are they before the throne of God, and serve him day and night in his temple; and He that sitteth on the throne shall dwell among them. They shall hunger no more, neither thirst any more; neither shall the sun light on them, nor any heat For the Lamb which is in the midst of the throne shall feed them, and shall lead them unto living fountains of waters; and God shall wipe away all tears from their eyes."

"The great tribulation," or persecution, of chapter vi. 9–11 may primarily be referred to, and the terms of the description are drawn from Old Testament prophecies. But from the winning revelation may be evolved the manifold teachings of God's word and of a sanctified experience as to the discipline of affliction

The Redeemer leads his people by tribulations through his kingdom on earth, and then introduces them to his kingdom in glory, from which every form of sorrow is for ever banished, and for which the earthly sorrows do a tender work of preparation.

Thus the purifying influence of afflictions in this life, and their preparative influence for the life to come, form one great work. They "refine" us in grace and for glory.

AFFLICTION'S SACRED ASSOCIATIONS.

1. Under the subduing influence of God's grace afflictions refine much of the happiness of earth by throwing new and sacred associations around its relationships.

When we are about to be deprived of a thing, or after we have lost it, new fountains of pleasure are opened up in it and burst forth from it. Deprivation bestows upon us a new source of happiness, tinged with sadness though the happiness may be.

Some of our purest enjoyments have their spring in sorrow, as out of the deep agony of anxiety on account of sin the regenerate soul rises, by faith, to rejoice in the Lord. Earth itself, and the things and persons of earth that are near and dear to us, are invested with increased beauty and interest by the very fact of our losing them.

"A dying man becomes aware that a peculiar beauty has been added to the beautiful scenes around him by the close approach of death. 'I owe,' says such a one, speaking of a scene which he was enjoying—'I owe to death itself half the beauty of this scene, and altogether owe to him the constant serenity with which I gaze upon it. Strange how the beauty and mystery of all Nature is heightened by the near prospect of that coming darkness which will sweep it all away! . . . What an air of freshness, of novelty and surprise does each old familiar object assume to me when I think of parting with it for ever!'

"Very true, very real, is this feeling (drawn from the much-suggesting *the night cometh*). We really do enjoy things more intensely because we know we are not to have them long. How well does experience certify that the most familiar scene grows new and strange to us when we are forthwith to leave it! The room in which we have sat day by day for years—rise to quit it for the last time, and we shall see something about its proportions, its aspect, that we never saw before. The little walk we have passed hundreds of times— how different everything beside it will seem when

we pass it silently, knowing that we shall do so
no more !" *

Much more strongly does this hold true of
what we have actually lost. The region of
memory is full of its sad pleasures which have
sprung from deep affliction.

Years ago you lost a little child. The heavy
blow almost broke your heart, for the infant was
the light of your eyes. A dark cloud rested upon
your home for a while, but it was slowly lifted,
and through it a light came down which even yet
irradiates your house. Ever and anon you steal
away to a secret drawer and gaze upon a little
lock of hair which you have carefully preserved.
Very tender recollections gush up in your mind.
The tear comes unbidden into your eye. But
you wipe it away, for you have ceased to mourn.
Through the vista of years the child-life appears
very beautiful. You remember its gleesome prat-
tle and its bounding vitality. And it is now
more beautiful, for it is bathed in the atmosphere
of heaven. You look at it through the light of that
better land. When you remember your toils and
your cares for it, you rejoice that it was your lot to
bestow them upon one who is no longer here, but

Leisure Hours in Town, p. 309.

with God. You think of the sufferings and the sins that it has escaped by being taken away so young, and you would not have it back. You look forward with the delightful anticipation of meeting it in heaven. God has transformed your grief into a most blessed joy. The death of that child has etherealized your life and drawn you nearer to God.

At an early age you lost a parent. The loss seemed to be irreparable. Fatherless, motherless, you knew not how you should get along in the world. But the memory of that deceased one has been ever with you as a sacred treasure, exercising perhaps a greater influence than would have been possessed by the loved one if still in the land of the living, and restraining you from many a sinful course to which you have been strongly tempted. The recollections of the translated are a source of strength and of tender joy to you.

> "God calls our loved ones, but we lose not wholly
>   What he has given;
> They live on earth in thought and deed as truly
>   As in his heaven."

Your house was once left unto you desolate by the departure from earth to heaven of one whom

14

you loved as your own soul. The blow was terrible, but what an effect it has had upon you! As you sit in the deepening twilight, and reproduce the image of the one whom you see not now, you invest the departed with heavenly attributes. You do not think of the faults which were once exhibited; death has transfigured them. You can say to God,

> " I trust he lives in thee, and there
> I find him worthier to be loved."

You recall the blissful associations of your united life. You think with gratitude of the offices of kindness which it was your privilege to discharge; if you ever inadvertently failed in any respect in tenderness, a chastened sorrow subdues you. The trial has made you better. You have the closest of all links, next to that which is connected with Jesus himself, to bind you to heaven. In your retirement and in your active life a heavenly incense surrounds you, the air of heaven breathes upon you, and you are prepared to say,

> " 'Tis better to have loved and lost
> Than never to have loved at all."

The past is no bleak desert in your memory.

It is a beautiful cloud-land, full of sacred associations. The golden flush of a clear sunset is upon it, and bathes the clouds that float over you in the most glorious of tints. Visions of beauty haunt your house and enter your heart, and reign over you with gentle sway.

Thus the sorrows of life, even those which are the severest of its tribulations, are tinged with joy, and the sadness and the gladness, inseparably interwoven in the Christian experience, enrich the life of earth, and prepare for the life of heaven from which the gloom shall be altogether banished. "Oh, satisfy us early with thy mercy," prays the Psalmist, "that we may rejoice and be glad all our days. Make us glad according to the days wherein thou hast afflicted us, and the years wherein we have seen evil." Ps. xc. 14, 15.

> " But how shall we be glad ?
> We that are journeying through a vale of tears,
> Encompassed with a thousand woes and fears,
>   How should we not be sad ?
>
> " Angels that ever stand
> Within the presence-chamber, and there raise
> The never-interrupted hymn of praise,
>   May welcome this command ;

"Or they whose strife is o'er,
Who all their weary length of life have trod,
As pillars now within the temple of God,
    That shall go out no more.

"But we who wander here,
We who are exiled in this gloomy place,
Still doomed to water earth's unthankful face
    With many a bitter tear,

"Bid us lament and frown,
Bid us that we go mourning all the day,
And we will find it easy to obey,
    Of our best things forlorn.

"Bid not that we be glad.
If it be true that mourners are the blest,
Oh leave us, in a world of sin, unrest
    And trouble, to be sad

" I spake, and thought to weep,
For sin and sorrow, suffering and crime,
That fill the world; all mine appointed time
    A settled grief to keep;

" When, lo! as day from night,
As day from out the womb of night forlorn,
So from that sorrow was that gladness born,
    Even in mine own despite.

" Yet was not that by this
Excluded at the coming of that joy;
Fled not that grief, nor did that grief destroy
    The newly-risen bliss.

" But side by side they flow,
Two fountains flowing from one smitten heart,
And ofttimes scarcely to be known apart—
    That gladness and that woe.

" Two fountains from one source,
Or which from two such neighboring sources run,
That aye for him who shall unseal the one
    The other flows perforce.

" And both are sweet and calm;
Fair flowers upon the banks of either blow;
Both fertilize the soil, and where they flow
    Shed round them holy balm."

SOFTEN THE ASPERITIES OF SOCIETY.

2. Afflictions soften the asperities of life, and thereby tone its social intercourse.

You have seen how anxious a man who thought he was approaching death was to be reconciled to those with whom he had been at enmity. He did not want to go down into the grave with the terrible malediction hanging over him: "If ye forgive not men their trespasses, neither will your heavenly Father forgive you." You have seen those who were at variance with him, and who had refused for years to enter his door, go to his bedside and speak a word of sympathy, and discharge offices of kindness for him.

In the dim twilight of sorrow many a rough point in the character, many an unseemly trait in the disposition, is unobserved. As you look into it while it settles down upon the house of a neighbor, you do not perceive the spots which the clear light of the sun made manifest. You only see a sick man lying upon the bed of suffering, or a ruined man deprived of his property, or a broken heart like Rachel weeping for her children and not willing to be comforted because they are not; and you gaze with pity. You cannot nourish any longer those harsh feelings which you had indulged. Perhaps you have been as much to blame as he. At all events, you will not add to his suffering by speaking of the past. You will rather try to lighten the load of the present by speaking kindly words to and about him. You are glad to find something good in him to talk about. All have their faults; and if God spares you while he lays the rod of suffering upon another, you will be charitable and pitiful.

Or if the twilight shades your own household, as you look through it upon the world, you become more loving toward it when you find that it walks softly beside you and gives you the tear of sympathy and the warm pressure of compas-

sion's hand. You feel that, notwithstanding the
depraving influence of sin, God has still, under
the subduing power of his grace, left us much
that breaks the force of the Fall. You have a
warmer side for those who are around you. It is
true that "a lying tongue hateth those that are
afflicted by it." Prov. xxvi. 28. This sometimes
happens. There have been men who injured
others, and then gloated with delight over the
suffering that they caused. But this conduct is
one of the most base meannesses of earth. The
mass of men turn away with disgust from the
wretch who exhibits it. The world looks with
scorn and contempt upon one who strikes a
defeated foe or heaps reproach upon an adver-
sary who has fallen into a low estate. It was
even a heathen injunction to speak well of
the dead. Sickness, sudden poverty, death, will
break down a wall of separation and increase the
amenities of life, if anything will do it. If they
have this effect upon men; if they make them
more kind, more gentle, more loving in their
intercourse; if they soften the heart, and cause
them to look more charitably upon each other,
and drive back the hasty word that might be
spoken, or quench the ill-feeling that might arise,

or banish it after it has arisen,—they have great reason to be thankful even for affliction.

Let it be borne in mind that sorrow, in some of its forms, will most certainly come to every family and to every individual. Live under the influence of that truth, and many an unkind thought, many a harsh feeling, many a hurtful act, will be prevented.* When affliction comes either upon you or upon those whom you may be tempted to deal with in an ungenerous manner, you will regret it if you have yielded to the temptation. Escape the sorrow by being ever courteous in the highest sense of the word.

What a change in the air of society would this single principle make if it were acted upon! What an important element of the heavenly atmosphere would it bring down to earth! What an educational influence would afflictions thus have for the blessed place which shall be shadowed by no sorrow!

PRODUCE MUTUAL SYMPATHY.

3. Afflictions fit us to sympathize with and comfort others who in their turn are afflicted.

* "If we could read the secret history of our enemies, we should find in each man's life sorrow and suffering enough to disarm all hostility."—Longfellow's *Table-Talk.*

The heart that has passed through the deep waters of tribulation is the most tender ; the voice that has itself cried with pain is the most gentle ; the hand that has suffered is the most soothing ministrant in the chamber of sorrow. The best sympathizer is one who has been a partaker in the same sufferings It is pre-eminently of Christian sufferers that this holds true. Hence the apostle Paul, speaking of himself, says, " God comforteth us in all our tribulation, that we may be able to comfort them which are in any trouble by the comfort wherewith we ourselves are comforted of God " 2 Cor. 1. 4. Those who have been sorely troubled, and in the midst of their sorrow have been comforted by God, are in turn the rich channels through which he distills his comfort into the hearts of other sufferers. Having felt the pain and having experienced the consolation, they best know when and how to apply that consolation to other stricken hearts. They can do it most gently and most surely

The Redeemer came under this rule. His sufferings on earth prepared him peculiarly for his position as a sympathizing high priest : " For in that he himself hath suffered, being tempted, he is able to succor them that are tempted." Heb. ii 18

Moreover, affliction not merely trains Christians to comfort others, but it increases their disposition to seek for the objects on which they may bestow their kind attentions. It develops their liberality in every good work. The apostle Paul thought it worthy of special mention in regard to the Church in Macedonia, "that in a great trial of affliction, the abundance of their joy, and their deep poverty, abounded unto the riches of their liberality." 2 Cor. viii. 2. We have all known persons who, in the very depth of deprivation and in unlooked-for increase of expenses, felt it to be a privilege to draw still more largely from their means for the help of charitable causes.

Let it be remembered that it is more blessed to give than to receive; that while you bestow happiness upon others you are yourself drinking deep of the Elysian spring; that the happiness which is not selfish, but which flows from the reaction upon ourselves of kindness done to others, is the highest happiness that a rational creature can enjoy, as it is one great element in the happiness of God, he, as a beneficent being, scattering blessings broadcast upon his creation and enjoying the work of his hands; and if, as the rolling billows of sorrow have appeared about

to overwhelm you, the great Comforter has come
down and made his grace sufficient for you, and
brought you up again purified through your tribulation, and led you out the better able to feel for
the children of sorrow and to do good to them,
thank God for your sufferings; they have opened
a new fountain of blessedness in your own being
which shall gush forth with a perennial flow
through all your course on earth, and then with
you mingle in the waters of the river of life that
for ever issue from the throne of God.

TEST OUR FAITH IN GOD.

4 Afflictions form a refining test of the reality
of our faith in God.

Almost any kind of a bark will sail in smooth
waters and with a favoring breeze; but when the
waves rush fiercely over the ocean, and the de-
stroying winds shriek around the masthead and
through the cordage, it is only a vessel that is
strong-ribbed and sound that can be depended
upon to ride out the storm.

It is comparatively easy to trust in God when
we are basking confidently in the smiles of his
favor and are not tossed about by any of the storms
of trouble; but when he seems to look upon us

with a frowning providence, and to send upon us the hailstones of his fierceness, it requires a deep trust indeed persistently to hold on to him. The faith of true believers sometimes quails in such circumstances, and they cry out, "Save, Master! we perish," and are met with the rebuke, "O ye of little faith, wherefore did ye doubt?" But by the very roughness of the storm the Christian character is developed.

The faith of Job was thus tested. On the supposition that he was not firmly established, Satan reasoned very strongly with the Lord when he said, "Doth Job fear God for naught? Hast thou not made a hedge about him, and about his house, and about all that he hath on every side? Thou hast blessed the work of his hands, and his substance is increased in the land. But put forth thine hand now, and touch all that he hath, and he will curse thee to thy face." Job i. 10–12. Then, in quick succession, sufferings of the most torturing kind are permitted to be brought upon the patriarch. His property is destroyed; his children are slain; a severe disease takes possession of his body; his wife, who should sustain him, tempts him to unbelief—"Dost thou still retain thine integrity? curse God and die;" his friends come and look upon him with sympathy, but intimate that he must have been guilty of secret sins, which men know not of, or God would not thus have permitted him to be dealt with. The balance trembles. The sufferer is sorely tried. A strong faith is needed to stand up under such multiform troubles. But Job has it; and his tribulations having accomplished the purpose of showing this, and also of bringing to light an element in his character of which he was not before conscious, he emerges from the furnace into a new career of prosperity, brilliant as the purest gold.

Trials show the stuff of which we are made. They exhibit to ourselves and to the world the strength and the grasp of our faith; for the essence of faith is that it peers above the seen and seizes hold of the unseen, and, however adverse all our surroundings may seem, still holds fast to God's assurance, and to the conviction that he will make all right in the end.

Because of this, the Church is in times of persecution purer than when she sits upon the heights of prosperity. Violent opposition separates the chaff from the wheat. Unworthy members will not largely cling to the organization when it brings nothing but trials. But those who feel that there is a reality in the truth which she embodies will hold on to it, and seize the inheritance at last, even though they must go through fire and blood to reach it.

Believers who suffer in the spirit of their religion know that their afflictions are not worthy to be compared with the glory which shall be revealed in them. They know that the Lord does not chastise willingly, but for their good, and that he is very pitiful and of tender mercy. Instead of being driven off, they are drawn the nearer to him; yea, they go the more implicitly to rest their head upon the bosom of Jesus, as the child, when sick and suffering, reposes with a deeper trust and a warmer affection in the arms of the mother. And from the blessed place they can cry out, "Sing, O heavens; and be joyful, O earth; and break forth into singing, O mountains: for the Lord hath comforted his people, and will have mercy upon his afflicted." Isaiah xlix. 13.

With the tendency to self-delusion that exists in the sinful soul, they have reason to rejoice whom God causes to pass through trials which show that they have a real faith and enable them to read their title clear to mansions in the skies.

" How different are summer storms from winter ones! In winter they rush over the earth with all their violence, and if any poor remnants of foliage or flowers have lingered behind, these are swept along at one gust. Nothing is left but desolation, and long after the rain has ceased pools of water and mud bear token of what has been. But when the clouds have poured out their torrents in summer, when the winds have spent their fury and the sun breaks forth again in its glory, all things seem to rise with renewed loveliness from their refreshing bath. The flowers, glistening with raindrops, smell sweeter than before; the grass seems to have gained another, brighter shade of green; and the young plants which had hardly come into sight have taken their place among their fellows in the borders, so quickly have they sprung up under the showers. The air, too, which may previously have been oppressive, is become clear and soft and fresh.

"Such, too, is the difference when the storms of affliction fall on hearts unrenewed by Christian faith and on those who abide in Christ. In the

former they bring out the dreariness and desolation which may before have been unapparent.
The gloom is not relieved by the prospect of any
cheering ray to follow it, of any flowers or fruit to
show its beneficence. But in the truly Christian
soul, though weeping endures for a night, joy
comes in the morning. A sweet smile of hope
and love follows every tear, and tribulation itself
is turned into the chief of blessings."*

But, in connection with the contrast thus so
beautifully drawn, it ought to be added that afflictions are often made the means of stopping sinners in their career of wickedness, and of bringing
them to thoughtfulness and to the amendment of
their ways. Thus it was with Manasseh. God
lays his hand heavily upon the wanderer, shows
him his nakedness and peril, and in the midst of
it leads him to cry out, "What must I do to be
saved?"

"Anguish is so alien to man's spirit that
nothing is more difficult to will than contrition.
Therefore, God is good enough to afflict us, that
our hearts, being brought low enough to feed on
sorrow, may the more easily sorrow for sin unto
repentance."

* *Guesses at Truth*, p. 476.

To any impenitent reader into whose hands this volume may fall I would say, If God were now to take from you some idol which is seated upon the throne of your heart and occupies your attention to the exclusion of him and his claims— if he were to break down your business, or over- turn your cup of pleasure, or mingle gall and bit- terness in your life, and if this were to have the effect of bringing you, as a broken-hearted peni- tent, to Christ—you would have reason throughout eternity to glorify him that he had thus dealt with you. Do you wish him so to do? Are you waiting to receive salvation at such a cost, or never to have it at all? Will nothing else lead you to Jesus but the loss of all that earth can give? If only that will do it, it would be mercy to you to pray that God would toss you about with the winds of destructive affliction, and so show you the illusory nature of all that belongs to earth, and impress upon your mind the reality of eternal things. But I would draw you to him by gentler means, and by the cords of love bind you, and all that you have, and all your strength of body and mind, to him and to his service. I would seek to win you in the spirit of these words:

15

" Jesus, take me for thine own ;
　To thy will my spirit frame ;
Thou shalt reign, and thou alone,
　Over all I have and am.

" Making thus the Lord my choice,
　I have nothing more to choose,
But to listen to thy voice
　And my will in thine to lose.

" Then, whatever may betide,
　I shall safe and happy be,
Still content and satisfied,
　Having all in having thee."

THE SANCTIFYING INFLUENCE.

5. Under the power of divine grace believers
are sanctified through afflictions.　Before the furnace the Lord sits as a refiner and purifier of
silver, and he purges them as gold and silver, that
they may offer unto him an offering in righteousness. Mal. iii. 3.　Suffering is a school in which
their knowledge is increased, their affections are
purified, their soul, in all its capacities and powers,
is strengthened.

JESUS PERFECTED BY SUFFERING.

Even sinless beings may be disciplined by trial.
The angels that fell not from their first estate, but

retained their purity in the hour of temptation, were doubtless made the stronger thereby. "As a man the Lord Jesus was disciplined by his sufferings, for he was subject to all the laws of sinless humanity; among others, to the gradual acquisition of knowledge, to the gradual heightening of character, and to this peculiar law, that information acquired by experience is invariably more vivid and permanent than that obtained by any other channel." *

Our Redeemer had the real twofold human nature "His development was a strictly human development. He did not come into the world endowed with infinite knowledge, but, as St. Luke tells us, ' He gradually advanced in wisdom.' He was not clothed with infinite power, but experienced the weaknesses and imperfections of human infancy. He grew as other children grow, only in a childhood of stainless and sinless beauty—' as the flower of roses in the spring of the year, and as lilies by the waters.' Ecclus. xxxix. 13, 14" †

The brief inspired statements about his early years—so pregnant with meaning as to the real

* William Archer Butler's *Sermons*, ii 79.
† Farrar's *Life of Christ*, 1 56

humanity that the Son of God assumed into
union with his divine person, in all respects soul
and body like our own, sinfulness excepted—are,
"The child grew, and waxed strong in spirit,
filled with wisdom; and the favor of God was
upon him;" "And Jesus increased in wisdom and
stature, and in favor with God and man." Luke
ii. 40, 52.

"His physical, mental and spiritual development was so natural and symmetrical that God
and man regarded his advancing and maturing
powers with increasing complacency. How suggestive is this simple statement! A child in
whose heart was bound up no 'folly' (Prov. xxii.
15); a young man pure in soul from all 'youthful
lusts' (2 Tim. ii. 22); a son whose consciousness
of his divine origin abated not his obedience to
earthly parents; a man so unpretending and
genial that his superior wisdom and unblemished
holiness conciliated the favor of others; a servant
of God ever mindful of his high destiny, yet
submissively working in obscurity at his mechan-
ical craft,—such we must suppose our Lord to
have been during the eighteen years of retirement
which his Father saw to be the best preparation

for his brief official life. And in all how perfect an example to all his followers!" *

In this human development suffering bore every relation to Jesus that it does to other men, except that sanctifying one which has a connection with the personal consciousness of sinful defilement. He illustrated what Chrysostom long ago said: " He who suffers for another not only benefits him, but becomes himself the more perfect."

Thus the inspired writer declares, " It became Him for whom are all things, and by whom are all things, in bringing many sons unto glory, to make the Captain of their salvation perfect through sufferings. For both He that sanctifieth and they who are sanctified are all of one. For which cause he is not ashamed to call them brethren, saying, I will declare thy name unto my brethren; in the midst of the Church will I sing praise unto thee. And again, I will put my trust in him. And again, Behold I and the children which God hath given to me. Forasmuch, then, as the children are partakers of flesh and blood, he also himself likewise took part of the same;

* I think this paragraph by Dr Angus is one of the most compactly suggestive and beautiful comments I have anywhere met.

that through death he might destroy him that had the power of death, that is, the devil, and deliver them who through fear of death were all their lifetime subject to bondage. For verily he took not on him the nature of angels; but he took on him the seed of Abraham. Wherefore, in all things it behoved him to be made like unto his brethren, that he might be a merciful and faithful High Priest in things pertaining to God, to make reconciliation for the sins of the people. For in that he himself hath suffered, being tempted, he is able to succor them that are tempted." Heb. ii. 10–18. And "in the days of his flesh, when he had offered prayers and supplications with strong crying and tears unto Him that was able to save him from death, and was heard in that he feared; though he were a son, yet learned he obedience by the things which he suffered; and being made perfect, he became the author of eternal salvation unto all them that obey him" Heb. v. 7–10.

In his vicarious relation, borne down by the tremendous weight of the guilt that had been transferred to him, and which the nearer he approached Calvary became the more horrid to his holy person, his human nature feared lest in its weakness it should sink under his agonies before his death, and mar the accomplishment of his great work. He prayed in the garden for preservation from this premature failure of his human powers of endurance, and in response to his petition an angel appeared from heaven strengthening him. Yea, more, there was united with that a shrinking from the death itself and a desire to escape it if it could be done—"If it be possible, let this cup pass from me." Just then, in a higher sense than applied to his disciples by himself, and One free from all blame, his spirit indeed was willing, but his flesh was weak. Through that struggle in the garden, which was the renewal of the conflict that had been waged in the wilderness of temptation, and the condensation of his life-warfare, he learned obedience or submission; not that he had been unsubmissive before, but there was then in him a mighty development of that grace. Especially was he, by the multiplied sufferings of his life, perfected as a sympathizer with his suffering people. "While we must believe that the divine omniscience, without an incarnation of the Son in human nature, would see and fully appreciate all the trials of the saints, and while we must believe that the divine mercy and pity are not less tender than those of a perfect man, since the divine is the source and pattern of the human, yet every believer feels how much more familiar and consoling is the sympathy of a Redeemer who is both God and our brother." *   "For we have not an high priest which cannot be touched with the feeling of our infirmities, but was in all points tempted like as we are, yet without sin." Heb. iv. 15.

A deepening and very tender touch is given to this truth by the fact that in his time of sore suffering Jesus also needed the sympathy of those whom he loved. For when he advanced to the struggle in Gethsemane he took with him his three favored disciples, that they might be within call in the intervals of the mighty spiritual conflict that had to be waged in a deeper loneliness and a deeper darkness into which they could not go. When he withdrew into the gloom of that, he asked them to watch with him. But on his return, looking for the needed human sympathy, he found them asleep. Then what a wail of disappointment there was in his words, "What! could ye not watch with me one hour?"!

* Sampson on Heb. ii. 17.

Strong and perfect and holy as he was, he yet needed sympathy. He felt the bitterness of the failure to find it. Therefore, he gives it the more tenderly now to those who seek it from him.

More strongly does this truth of the disciplinary nature of suffering hold true of sinful creatures, who, in addition to being developed and strengthened in their character, need to be purified from the dross of sin.

Suffering itself does not produce any sanctifying result. Pain does not tend to the production of holiness. Ascetic mortification of the body will not kill the sin of the soul. It is the way in which suffering is endured, and the influence of the Spirit that accompanies it, which accomplish the object. A fourfold influence may herein be distinguished.

CAUSE THE EVIL OF SIN TO BE FELT.

(1.) Afflictions make us feel in a peculiarly sensitive manner the evil of sin as the cause of all suffering.

The Lord often chastens his people to produce in them this consciousness, that they may be led to abandon all sin and escape its eternal penalty. This is true of the pains which are brought on them by particular transgressions: "When we are judged, we are chastened of the Lord that we should not be condemned with the world." 1 Cor. xi. 32. Much more does it hold true of other sorrows.

The most vivid descriptions of a battlefield can give no adequate idea of its horrors. Those who have walked over one before the smoke of the roaring batteries has fully blown away, and gazed upon the mangled bodies, and heard the moans of the wounded, and helped to bury the headless, limbless dead, have received impressions of the miseries of war such as others have never had.

You may read of afflictions. You may even gaze upon them at your side. So long, however, as you are free from the touch of them, you do not feel their peculiar bitterness. But they roll in sharply upon you. Sickness seizes hold upon your body. In the morning you say, Would God it were even! and in the evening, Would God it were morning! Or the messenger of death takes your child, your husband, your wife, and leaves your house unto you desolate. This is the work of sin. You feel it now. If sin had not entered it, the world would have been one everlasting Paradise of health and of joy. Family circles would never have been broken.   The pang of pain would never have been felt.   But the destroyer comes.   As his wild waves are rushing on toward the deep black gulf of death, he is continually tossing up the seethings of his ruin, bitter foretastes of eternal woes.   You start back from the prospect.   You see sin to be exceeding sinful. Rom. vii. 13.   You are led to a deeper hatred of it, and—if faithful to your own souls—to the earnest prayer, God deliver me both from its pollution and its pain !   Personal affliction, the effect of sin, intensifies personal abhorrence of it.   And a thorough hatred of sin (resulting not merely, it is true, from a perception of its painful effects, but united with the fact that it is odious because of its relation to God) is a most important factor in the sanctification of the soul and its preparation for the glory of heaven.

It must not be understood from this that the sufferings of men in this life are a test by which we can judge of the degree of their sinfulness. " Many are the afflictions of the righteous." Ps. xxxiv. 19.   The greatest sufferers in this world have not been the greatest sinners.   On the contrary, some of the most pious characters who are brought before us in the word of God endured the heaviest tribulations.   The Psalms especially are

full of references to the sorrows which come upon
the people of God; and because of that, they
palpitate with the conviction of sin, and therefore are peculiarly fitted to be a manual of devotion in all ages. God does permit his people to
suffer here, but when the suffering has accomplished its purpose, he delivers them from it and
bestows upon them an infinite compensation for it
all. On the other hand, he sometimes lets the
wicked go on in prosperity, but they treasure up
unto themselves wrath against the day of wrath;
and the future shall be the more severe because
of the prosperity which they had, but trifled with
and used against God.

MAKE CONSCIENCE SENSITIVE TO TRANSGRESSIONS.

2 But though afflictions are not tests of character, nor are particular sufferings always the results
of particular transgressions, they are made the
occasions of bringing the individual iniquities of
believers more clearly to their sensitive consciousness. The light of an increased and tender
thoughtfulness, of increased reading of the Bible,
of increased prayer, is through them concentrated
upon their souls. This shows the sufferers more
clearly the sins for which they should prostrate

themselves before God in the deepest humility, and place themselves anew beneath the blood of sprinkling. It shines into the innermost chambers of the heart's imagery (Ezek. viii. 12), and from the most secret corners and the darkest recesses brings up the actions of the past and arraigns them at the bar of God.

Christian sufferer! you remember how this process went on in your case after you had recovered a little from the first weight of some blow that once came upon you. There was a thoughtful wandering of your mind over the past. You saw in a new light your ungrateful neglect of God's mercies, your failures in duty, your infirmities of disposition, the shallowness of your repentance, the smallness of your faith. You did not turn away from the sight. You did not try to evade the force of the charges which an enlightened conscience brought against you. Nay, you uttered self-accusations. You were ready to say, " Depart from me ; for I am a sinful man, O Lord." Luke v. 8.* But you

* How much to the life that exclamation of Peter was! How often does it appear, even on the lower ground of the dealings of men with each other, as in the feelings of one who is conscious that he is not fit for the companionship of a high

turned to the precious word, and there found
what encouraged you. You were able to say
with the Psalmist, " This is my comfort in my
affliction: for thy word hath quickened me." Ps.
cxix. 50. Unless that had been your delight you
would have perished. Ps. cxix. 92. It deepened
your sense of guilt, and showed you many respects in which you had come short of obedience to God. But you also found a rare beauty
and fullness in it which you had never seen
before. Old familiar passages became invested
with increased power and brilliancy. Truths that

and noble-minded friend and benefactor, and yet would not for
the world be deprived of it! Farrar, in his brilliant *Life of
Christ*, i. 243, finely says · " A flash of supernatural illumina-
tion had revealed to Peter both his own sinful unworthiness and
who *He* was who was with him in the boat. It was the cry of
self-loathing which had already realized something nobler. It
was the first impulse of fear and amazement, before they had
time to grow into adoration and love. St. Peter did not *mean*,
' Depart from me;' he only meant—and this was known to the
Searcher of hearts—' I am utterly unworthy to be near thee, yet
let me stay.' How unlike was this cry of his passionate and
trembling humility to the bestial ravings of the unclean spirits,
who bade the Lord to let them alone, or to the hardened degra-
dation of the filthy Gadarenes, who preferred to the presence of
their Saviour the tending of their swine!"

had escaped your notice before shone forth with the most soothing and cheering light Rich jewels, lustrous with the reflection of heaven, seemed to sparkle all over the sacred pages. You rejoiced in them as one that had found great spoil. The promises were exceeding great and precious, and you laid hold of them as belonging to you. As Luther said of himself, you never understood many passages of the Bible until you looked at them through affliction. It was delightful to turn over the leaves of the oracles of God and hear the gentle voice with which he spake to you Then, as you bent over the book, the incense of prayer most sweetly went up from your contrite heart. You prayed as you never prayed before for the forgiveness of your sins, for the increase of God's grace to you, for his strength to bring you out of darkness, and for a speedy translation from this sorrowful world to the presence of the glorified Redeemer. The result of it all was a deepening humility of soul. You felt very tender in the presence of God. You prostrated yourself with a humble and contrite heart before him. With such he has promised to dwell (Isa. lvii. 15), and you felt your need of him. Was there not a blessed-

ness in this? Do you not feel the effects of it
still?

"When around us lie shattered the hopes and
dreams of fleeting prosperity, when we walk
among ruins, ourselves a ruin, then God's time
is near; his hand is busy in that chaos; the
broken heart is there which he has promised not
to spurn; and his Spirit, which works by means
and times and seasons, is even now about to
weave of the dark substance of that grief the
garment of praise of which his prophet has
spoken, the adorning meet for the everlasting
kingdom. Blessed indeed are the mourners to
whom their mourning has brought humiliation!
the raptures of eternity will declare whether that
is a repentance to be repented of." *

From deep humiliation of spirit, produced by
sanctified thoughtfulness, prayer and the reading
of the word, the believer rises to a higher stand-
ard of holiness, to a more jealous guarding of his
heart, to a more intense activity for God. " Before
I was afflicted I went astray; but now have I
kept thy word," said the Psalmist. Ps. cxix. 67.
Since his day multitudes have had occasion to
repeat the assertion.

* William Archer Butler's *Sermons*, ii. 75, 76.

WEAN FROM THE WORLD.

(3.) Afflictions wean believers from the world and lead them to more heartfelt desires after the presence of God. They show the perishable and uncertain nature of all that is had here, and by contrast turn the attention to the unending duration of the heavenly bliss. "For our light affliction, which is but for a moment, worketh for us a far more exceeding and eternal weight of glory; while we look not at the things which are seen, but at the things which are not seen; for the things which are seen are temporal, but the things which are not seen are eternal." 2 Cor. iv. 17, 18.

"One stroke of sorrow carries with it, as it were, the condensed experience of years, and impresses with a truth, a depth, a reality, never before known the great fact that our pulpits are for ever publishing, and for ever publishing in vain, that the world is a traitor to our hopes, that its word is falsehood, its promises mockery; that however in the calm summer day we may float in lazy security upon its surface, it inevitably whelms us when the wind rises." *

It is well for many that this is so. They would

* William Archer Butler's *Sermons*, ii. 76.

16

become very thoughtless creatures if their life flowed on in one uninterrupted stream of enjoyment. If the friends, the possessions and the pleasures of earth had impressed upon them a permanent value, even the heir of glory would grow too much attached to things seen. They would occupy all his attention. He would not toil in the requisite preparation for heaven. Therefore, as, entranced with the allurements of earth, he stands upon the brink of ruin, and knows not that he is there, the heavenly Father dashes his hand across them, and they disappear from sight or are mingled in one mass of confused sorrow. In his sudden bereavement the fascinated one starts from his dangerous position, and, by his affliction rescued from ruin, with a deepened interest anticipates the lasting, the pure, the unbroken.*   From

* The expressions of this paragraph were suggested by the following incident, which I met somewhere in the corner of a newspaper: Two painters were employed to fresco the walls of a cathedral. Both stood on a rude scaffolding some distance from the floor. One was so intent upon his work that, forgetting where he was, he stepped back slowly, surveying critically the work of his brush, until he had neared the edge of the plank on which he stood. Another step in his rapt unconsciousness would have cast him down. At this moment his companion, perceiving his danger, and knowing that to speak to him would precipitate his fall, seized a wet brush and flung it against the wall, spatter-

the sorrows of earth there springs an increased
desire for heaven ; so that the Christian can say,

> " As link by link was rent away,
>   My heart wept blood, so sharp the pain;
> But I have learned to count this day
>   That temporal loss eternal gain;
> For all that once detained me here
> Now draws me to a holier sphere—
>   A holier sphere, a happier place,
> Where I shall know as I am known,
>   And see my Saviour face to face,
> And meet rejoicing round his throne
> The faithful souls made perfect there
> From earthly stains and mortal care "

It is really a blessing for immortal souls to
have some of the links that bind them to earth
taken up to heaven ; to have weakness and pain
of body, if it will draw them nearer to that land
where there is no pain, and where the inhabitant
never says, I am sick ; to be brought into such a
position that, with the possessions of earth van-
ishing from view and with the heart set on the
things of heaven, every affliction, light compared

ing the picture with unsightly blotches of coloring. The painter
flew forward with the natural purpose of saving his work, and
thereby saved himself. Then he turned upon his friend, at first
with fierce upbraidings ; but when apprised of the danger that
he had escaped, he blessed the rough act that had saved him

with the glory of the better land, momentary compared with its unending duration, shall be the means of increasing the joys of salvation. If tribulation will bring you into this position—if it will win you more and more from the perishable enjoyments of this world, and keep your eye, with anxious desire, intently fixed on heaven, while the importunate question bursts from the heart, How long, O Lord? how long?—if it will excite you to more active preparation for the holiness and blessedness of the upper sanctuary,—then you will have occasion to say, "It is good for me that I have been afflicted." Ps. cxix. 71.

DEEPEN CHRISTIAN GRACES.

(4.) After what has been said, it is easy to see that sanctified afflictions deepen and bring out into a clearer light all Christian graces; "and grace is glory in the bud; glory is grace in the flower." As the apostle says, "We glory in tribulations also; knowing that tribulation worketh patience, and patience experience, and experience hope; and hope maketh not ashamed, because the love of God is shed abroad in our hearts by the Holy Ghost, which is given unto us." Rom. v. 3–5. It is not hard to be patient in tribulation,

under the living influence of things unseen and
of their connection with the discipline of earth.
With the heavenly glory clearly before us we can
bear up under temporary ills. The hope of the
future enables us patiently to submit; and that in
turn strengthens our hope and buoys us up as we
are borne on toward the cloudless clime. The
trying of our faith worketh patience; and that
has a perfect work which will make us perfect
and entire, wanting nothing. James i. 3, 4.
Earnestly looking toward heaven, the believer is
increasingly prepared for it. His sense of de-
pendence upon God is deepened. His faith in
the divine promises is increased. His repentance
for his sins becomes of a more tender, more soul-
subduing kind. He loves God the more because
of the chastening hand which he lays upon him
for his purification; and out of the depths he
waiteth for the Lord more than they watch
for the morning. Ps. cxxx. 6. The ravishing
views of heavenly blessedness which he sometimes has leads him to say, "I have a desire to
depart and to be with Christ, which is far better." Phil. i. 13. He becomes prepared to leave
the earth, and to have its most tender associations severed without a pang; for up above are

more alluring scenes, and he would be absent from the body, with all that may be attractive around it, so that he may be present with the Lord. Weary months of suffering cause him to turn the eye full upon the heavenly orb. He will not rush uncalled into the glorified presence of the Redeemer. All the days of his appointed time on earth will he wait until his change come. Job xiv. 14. Yet there will be about him a holy impatience that sends up the prayer, "Come, Lord Jesus, come quickly!"

> "My home is in heaven, my rest is not here;
> Then why should I murmur when trials are near?
> Be hushed, my dark spirit; the worst that can come
> But shortens my journey and hastens me home.

> "It is not for me to be seeking my bliss
> And building my hopes in a region like this;
> I seek for a city which hands have not piled,
> I pant for a country by sin undefiled."

Thus intimate is the connection which the Bible shows to exist between sanctified sorrows and glory. The Lord "himself connects the suffering and the reward in that question to the wondering disciples, ' Ought not Christ to have suffered these things and to enter into his glory?' Luke xxiv. 26. And St. Peter in like manner combines the same double aspect of the office of the Redeemer, 'the sufferings of Christ and the glory that shall follow' (I Pet. i. 11), declaring them both equally the subject of ancient prophecy." * In virtue of their union with him, it is said of believers that the sufferings of Christ abound in them. 2 Cor. i. 5. With them, too, the glory is connected, for "if they suffer with him, they shall also be glorified together." Rom. viii. 17.† For the present, afflictions are not joyous but grievous. The believer looks not upon them as a stoic. He will be no ascetic, deliberately bringing suffering upon himself. "The Bible does not teach either by precept or example that Christians are to bear pain as though it were not pain, or bereavements as though they caused no sorrow. Unless real afflictions prove real sorrows, they will not produce the fruits of sorrow." The body and the mind of believers are as sensitive as those of unbelievers. The throb of pain will be as

* William Archer Butler, i. 77.

† " Life is energy of Love,
Divine or human, exercised in pain,
In strife and tribulation, and ordained,
If so approved and sanctified, to pass
Though shades and silent rest to endless joy."
Wordsworth's *Excursion*, book v.

keenly felt by them, the tears of anguish will gush as freely from their eyes, as in the case of sensitive persons of the world who have no hope to sustain them in their punishment. But the glory that is to be revealed shines through the tears, and underlies the pain, and dispels the darkness, and enables believers to rejoice, inasmuch as they are partakers of Christ's sufferings, that when his glory shall be revealed they may be glad with exceeding joy. 1 Pet. iv. 13. "The Spirit itself beareth witness with our spirit that we are the children of God; and if children, then heirs; heirs of God, and joint-heirs with Christ; if so be that we suffer with him, that we may be also glorified together. For I reckon that the sufferings of this present time are not worthy to be compared with the glory which shall be revealed in us." Rom. viii. 16–18.

Therefore, Christian disciple, when God in his providence permits tribulations to beat upon you, murmur not. Consider the divine Being who endured such afflictions while working out your redemption, and be not weary or faint in your mind. "Whatever be the intensity of sorrow that bows and oppresses the heart of man, remember that for every grief you suffer the meek

and holy One suffered a thousand; that there is
not, in the spirit, a dungeon or recess of anguish,
however untrodden or lonely, in which the Lord
of glory was not an inhabitant before you. Does
the victim know the loss of earthly comforts?
Christ knew not where to lay his head. Does he
regret the fall from wealth or power? **Let** him
remember who it was that emptied himself of the
glory which he had before the world was, and left
the throne of the universe for a life of poverty
and the agonies of Calvary. Does he deplore
the loss of friends? Christ was friendless in his
most trying hour. Does he bewail the ingrati-
tude of friends? Christ was betrayed by his own
familiar ones. Finally, does he fear the coming
of death, the torture of separation? What death
can he anticipate which shall approach the horror
of the last days of his Redeemer? Thus, wherever we turn, whatever be our shade of grief, we
are but feeble copyists of the great Sufferer who
in his own person exhausted every variety of
human sorrow." * Amid all the storms that arise
as you voyage homeward, he is in the vessel with
you, directing your course. You shall be safely
steered clear of all breakers, and go bounding

* William Archer Butler's *Sermons,* ii. 78.

over all the waves, and at last moor in the haven
of perpetual peace and joy.

> " The light of smiles shall fill again
>   The lids that overflow with tears,
> And weary hours of woe and pain
>   Are promises of happy years.
> There is a day of sunny rest
>   For every dark and troubled night,
> And grief may bide an evening guest,
>   But joys shall come with early light.
> For God has marked each sorrowing day,
>   And numbered every secret tear;
> And heaven's long age of bliss shall pay
>   For all its children suffer here."

VI.

THE judgment throne stands upon the border-line between time and eternity. The vestibule of the grave opens immediately into the mighty hall in which the everlasting destiny of men is authoritatively declared. What, then, is the relation in which our daily conduct here stands to that solemn transaction? What the relation which its sentence bears to the eternal state beyond? The fleeting moments as they pass along; the thoughts that come and go, almost as evanescent as the changeful shadows of an evening cloud; the affections that burn within us; the habits that control us; the lives that we live,—what have they to do with the judgment day and with the future worlds? Do the effects which they produce pass away with them? Or do they write down in advance the sentence which is to be uttered against us?

THE PRINCIPLE OF THE JUDGMENT.

The apocalyptic seer in one of his final visions beheld, in act, the answer to these questions, and in another he heard the great Judge announce it from the throne in warning words.

"I saw," he says, "a great white throne, and Him that sat on it, from whose face the earth and the heaven fled away; and there was found no place for them. And I saw the dead, small and great, stand before God; and the books were opened. and another book was opened, which is the book of life: and the dead were judged out of those things which were written in the books, *according to their works.*" Rev. xx. 11, 12.

"And," declared the Judge, "behold I come quickly; *and my reward is with me, to give every man according as his work shall be.*" Rev. xxii. 12.

Thus in the divine administration the principle prevails which is recognized in human governments. In the future worlds men shall receive precisely what is their due, and "there will be a great distinction in the recompense which the different members of each class shall receive." Not merely is the whole human race divided into two great classes, one of whom rise to the perfect holiness and happiness of the saved, and the other sink to the sin and misery of the lost; not only shall the pearly gate of the celestial city be opened for the admission of those who have believed in the Redeemer, have had their guilt washed away in the blood of the atonement and their hearts purified by the indwelling of the Spirit, and thus have been fitted for the holy employments of heaven, while those who obey not God and reject the gospel of our Lord Jesus Christ shall be visited with destruction from the presence of the Lord and from the glory of his power (2 Thess. i. 9); not merely are the saints to be saved and unreconciled sinners condemned, —but the measure of the happiness or of the misery which each shall receive is to be according to the life here.

The Scriptures give no countenance to the idea that all sinners of different shades of moral character are looked upon by God with the same measure of disapprobation. "Every sin," it is true, "deserveth God's wrath and curse, both in this life and that which is to come;" and in reference to their acceptance with God, all men, as sinners, do stand on a level. But it is also true that "some sins in themselves, and by reason of several aggravations, are more heinous in the sight of God than others," and, being more heinous, call down the more severe marks of his displeasure.

REWARDS ACCORDING TO EARTHLY WORKS.

Nor, on the other hand, do the heirs of heaven stand on the same plane. Here, again, it is true that as far as their justification is concerned they are equal. But there are measures of blessedness connected with the use which the justified make of their opportunities. Heaven is the reward of the Redeemer's work, but the measure of the reward to each of the redeemed is according to the life on earth.

There are apparent difficulties in the way of this truth which lead some to have a hazy apprehension of it, and to be encouraged in a professed Christian life which is very formal and very fruitless for their own souls and for God.

CONSISTENT WITH PERFECTION OF CHRIST'S WORK.

It may be objected that the assertion, that in heaven some of the redeemed occupy a higher position and enjoy a greater degree of blessedness than others, militates against the perfection of Christ's redeeming work. As he poured out the same blood, endured the same sufferings, died upon the same cross, and thus finished the same satisfaction for them all, ought we not to expect that every one will receive precisely the same benefits?

This, however, proceeds upon an erroneous view of the atonement. The application of its blessings depends upon the design of God; a discrimination in the bestowal of those blessings does not detract from the value and the merit of Christ's work. On account of the dignity of the divine Redeemer's person that value is infinite It was sufficient not merely to have saved all the sinners of mankind, but all the sinners of all worlds. But it had no reference to the fallen angels; they did not come within its provisions. Nor was it designed to save those men who go on in their sin and finally sink into the abode of the lost. To assert that it did embrace them, and that God fails in his purpose, is as irreverent and derogatory to his character and perfections as the limitation of the value of Christ's work would be depreciatory of the dignity of his person. Redemption had a special reference to that seed whom, in eternity, the Father gave to the Son.

But the giving of this definite character to it did not depreciate its price nor detract from the perfection of Christ's satisfaction.

It is a further application of this principle to say that redemption having this definite character, it is entirely consistent with it to suppose that the time when, and the extent to which, its blessings shall be conferred upon those who come within its provisions may be different in different cases. We find this to be the case. By his atoning work Christ secured not only eternal life for all his people, but all that is necessary to prepare them for it. The gift of the Spirit to lead them to the exercise of faith and repentance, and the continued influence of the Spirit in the process of sanctification, are the reward of Christ's righteousness, bestowed upon his people on account of what he has done. Are we, then, to suppose that as he paid the same ransom-price for them all, this influence must come upon them in the same manner, at the same period of life and to the same extent? Were they all delivered from condemnation and justified from eternity when the covenant was made? Were they even justified when Jesus died and thereby fulfilled the condition of the covenant? No; they are born children of wrath, under condemnation, as others are. Justification comes not upon them until they believe and are converted Their belief, with their attendant justification, was secured from eternity; but they receive not the one actually until they exercise the other. Again: do they all believe at the same period of life, and thus remain only the same length of time under condemnation, and spend the same period on earth in a justified state? No, some are drawn to the Redeemer in youth, some in the prime of manhood, some not until old age. The third, the sixth, the ninth, the eleventh hours have their representatives in justification. Yet again: are all the redeemed delivered as rapidly, and in the same stages of life as completely, from the evil consequences of sin here? No; in some the work of sanctification is commenced sooner, and carried on more quickly, than in others. Some are, through the tender mercy of God, preserved from transgressions which bring upon others who, have committed them, the severest sufferings of this life.

There are, then, differences here in the bestowal of the blessings of redemption. Now, if we believe, in conformity with what appears to be the teaching of the Bible, that, in the eternal life which all the redeemed receive, different positions are assigned to them and different degrees of blessedness enjoyed by them, and that these are bound up with the mode in which the earthly life is spent, we do not derogate from the infinite value of the Redeemer's work; we only extend to the hereafter what is evidently God's rule in dealing here.

This agrees with the analogy of the effect of the first sin. As in the covenant of redemption Christ was the representative of his people, so in the covenant of works Adam was the representative of all his descendants. The latter half of the fifth chapter of the Epistle to the Romans runs the comparison between the two. The sin of Adam brought the whole race equally under condemnation, and into a state of spiritual death and inward corruption, its consequence; but as far as the evils resulting from this are concerned, there are very great differences among men. The sinful defilement exhibits itself in a more odious form in some than in others. God, in his providence and grace, places some in a position where it is checked and restrained, and thus they do not in so great a degree suffer from its

painful effects. So Christ, as the representative
of his people, procured eternal life for them all;
but the provisions of the covenant are such that
in the enjoyment of that life in heaven there will
be different degrees of blessedness connected with
the preparation on earth for it.

NOT THE PAPAL DOGMA OF GOOD WORKS.

Again: it may be feared that this doctrine will
impregnate the grace of God with an erroneous
view of the merit of good works. Romanists do
misinterpret the rule, and weave into it a statement derogatory to the sacrifice of Christ, by
assigning the highest places in heaven "to those
who have performed works of supererogation, by
doing more than was strictly enjoined them by
the law." But there are no such works. There
is no one who does more than is enjoined; for
says the Saviour himself, "After ye shall have
done all these things which are commanded you,
say, We are unprofitable servants; we have done
that which was our duty to do." Luke xvii. 10.

NO IMPERFECTION IN HEAVEN.

Further, there might be danger of drawing the
inference that "the state of those who have the

least degree of blessedness would be imperfect in
its kind, or have something in it which would
abate their happiness, or be the occasion of envy
or uneasiness, as the superior excellences of some
in this imperfect state often appear to be."

If either of these objections could fairly be
made, it would form a strong reason against our
reading of the Bible in this respect. But they
arise from a misapprehension of the truth.   And
here, as is generally the case, a clear statement of
the truth itself, with the evidence on which it is
based, will obviate the objections by showing that
there is nothing in it to which they can apply.

THE TRUE VIEW.

Let it be observed, then, that while the rewards
given to the righteous are *according* to their
works, they are not *for* their works. There is a
great difference between the two expressions.   It
sometimes happens that out of the affection that
one friend bears to another, he, on account of
some good deed that the other has done, takes
his children into special favor, deals gently with
their faults, and wherever he can find anything
to commend gives them a suitable reward according to what they have done. This does not fully

express the relation that exists between the eternal Father and the Son with his people. But it enables us to see that while the redeeming work of the Son is the only obedience that in itself deserves heaven, yet that, in consequence of the relation which his people bear to him, they may be looked upon through the light of his merit, so that God for his sake forgives their sins, and is graciously pleased to proportion their enjoyment of the purchased reward to their conduct.

The deeds of believers do not in themselves merit anything from God. As far as their acts are holy they are due to the Spirit of God, and they continue through life to be imperfect and to need the blood of sprinkling to purify them from their guilt. In view of their entrance into the holy place, the language which God may address to them is, "Not for your sakes do I this, be it known unto you: be ashamed and confounded for your own ways." Ezek. xxxvi. 32. The most advanced believers that have ever walked the earth have confessed that even their best deeds were tainted with imperfection. To the end they needed forgiveness. When the redeemed arrive in the presence of the Lamb above, every crown is cast at his feet, and from the whole number the song goes up, "Not unto us, not unto us, but unto thy name give glory." Ps. cxv. 1. "It is through the dying love of Christ that the way is opened for the consistent communication of divine blessedness to guilty creatures:" and all happiness flows to us through him Not merely the forgiveness of sins, but all subsequent blessings in grace and glory, are the rewards of his righteousness. Believers are, however, entitled to the blessedness which they receive. On account of the union between Christ and them he suffered the punishment that was due to them; and, accepted in the Beloved, their works are accepted likewise, their imperfection is overlooked, and whatever is good in them is rewarded.

We often see comparatively worthless stones which receive a great value from their precious setting. The believer's works derive all their worth from the righteousness of Jesus in which they are set, and in which the eye of God looks upon them. It is in the censer of his intercession that they are presented in the heavenly court The richer they are, the greater the reward that shall be received 'Like those stars which have no light in themselves, but only reflect that which comes from their sun, all their brightness in the presence of God is derived from the Sun of righteousness; and as some stars shine brighter and occupy a more prominent position in the firmament than others, so it is in the kingdom of glory.

Moreover, "such actions only as flow from grateful love to God and Christ can be consistently rewarded, for these virtues only are recognized by Scripture as having any good desert. One who does good from impure motives has, as Christ says, already received his reward."

In every degree of happiness with which the hearts of his people throb, the Redeemer sees of the travail of his soul. For them he has purchased heaven For them he has secured the means by which they are prepared for the participation in its glory. All that they possess, from the first pulsation of joy in the new heart on through the soul-satisfying thrill of eternity, is due to him.

Of the direct and positive revelations which are made in the Bible in reference to the varied life of heaven and the degrees of its happiness, the following both afford proofs and contain teachings as to the lives that lead to the greater degrees of bliss.

GRADATIONS OF ANGELS.

1. There is nothing inconsistent with true views of heaven in the supposition that different positions may be occupied by its inhabitants, for the Scriptures teach that there are gradations or ranks among the angels.

The Bible does not go as far as the Romanists or Jews on this point. Some of the Jewish rabbis held that there were seven heavens, each with its own order of angels. Romanists very precisely erect the angels into a hierarchy, and divide them into three classes.*

The sum of the teaching of the Bible on the subject is found in such passages as Eph. i. 20, 21 : God raised Christ " from the dead, and set him at his own right hand in the heavenly places, far above all principality, and power, and might, and dominion, and every name that is named, not only

---

* The only foundation that they have for this is found in a spurious Epistle attributed to Dionysius the Areopagite, who is mentioned in Acts xvii 34 as a convert under Paul's ministry ; which Epistle, however, is demonstrated to be a forgery, composed perhaps four hundred years after the death of its reputed author. The object which they have in view in making such a division is to endeavor to find in it a heavenly basis on which their unscriptural government may rest.

in this world, but also in that which is to come ;"
Col. i. 16: "For by him were all things created
that are in heaven and that are in earth, visible
and invisible, whether they be thrones, or dominions, or principalities, or powers" The context
shows that by "principalities," "powers," "might,"
"dominions," angels are meant; and these terms
seem to indicate different ranks of angels.

"In all departments of Nature there is a regular gradation from the lower to the higher forms
of life; from the almost invisible vegetable fun-
gus in plants to the cedar of Lebanon; from the
minutest animalcule to the gigantic mammoth. In
man we meet with the first, and to all appearances
the lowest, of rational creatures. That he should
be the only creature of his order is, *a priori*, as
improbable as that insects should be the only
class of irrational animals. There is every reason
to presume that the scale of being among rational
creatures is as extensive as that in the animal
world. The modern philosophy which deifies
man leaves no room for any order of beings
above him. But if the distance between God
and man be infinite, all analogy would prove that
the orders of rational creatures between us and
God must be inconceivably numerous. As this is

in itself probable, it is clearly revealed in the Bible to be true." "These holy angels are evidently not all of the same rank. This appears from the terms by which they are designated—terms which imply diversity of order and authority. Some are princes, others potentates, others rulers of the world." *

If the society of the unfallen intelligences be "composed of members of unequal dignity, power and excellence," some of whom are even peculiarly exalted as chiefs and rulers, it is certainly analogical, and it cannot be unscriptural, to suppose that restored and glorified men shall also be graded in the kingdom of heaven. But the gradation shall not be marred by the inequalities which in this stage of our existence are the result of the force, fraud, chicanery and intrigue which too often exalt the least worthy and depress the most excellent, not only in the world, but even in the Church. It shall be based on intellectual and moral grounds, shall be according to truth and equity, and shall be the development and reward of faithfulness in this life. "The law which connects the actings of boyhood or of youth with the character of manhood is the identical, the

* Dr. Charles Hodge's *Systematic Theology*, i. 637, 639.

unrepealed law which connects our actings in time with our character through eternity. The way in which the moral discipline of youth prepares for the honors and the enjoyments of a virtuous manhood is the very way in which the moral and spiritual discipline of a whole life prepares for a virtuous and happy immortality. . . . The law of moral continuity between the different stages of human life is also the law of continuity between the two worlds." * And under that law redeemed souls pass into the world of the glorified with their sinless inequalities in existence and in action.

All men are created equal in the rights that belong to humanity. But mental and active sameness and equality do not exist among them in their birth or in their growth. "In this life God has very wisely allotted various capacities, powers and talents, in different ways and degrees, to different men, according to the various ends for which he designs them and the business on which he employs them. There is not the least reason to suppose that God will abolish this variety in the future world; it will rather continue there in all its extent. We must suppose, then,

* Chalmers's Sermon on *Heaven a Character.*

that there will be, even in the heavenly world, a
diversity of tastes, of labors and of employments,
and that to one person this, to another that field
in the boundless kingdom of truth and of useful
occupation will be assigned for his cultivation,
according to his peculiar powers, qualifications
and tastes. . . . At least such arrangements will
doubtless be made by God in the future life that
each individual will there develop more and more
the germs implanted within him by the hand of
the Creator, and will be able, more fully than he
ever could do here, to satisfy the wants of his intellectual nature, and thus to make continual progress in the knowledge of everything worthy of
being known, of which he could only learn the
simplest elements in this life; and he will be able
to do this in such a way that the increase of
knowledge will not be detrimental to piety, as it
often proves on earth, but rather promotive of
it." *   The active powers which are trained here
will also have freer scope and wider fields for
their exercise.

Hence, as we shall see a little farther on, the
differences of faculties, of opportunities, of faith-

* McClintock & Strong's *Cyclopædia,* article " Heaven," from
Knapp's *Theology.*

fulness in this world have much to do, under the
simple law of development, with the standing
of souls in the glorious world.

But let us not hesitate to admit the sovereignty
and good pleasure of God therein also. The
enjoyment of salvation itself, and the distribution
of many of its blessings, are bestowed on the
election of God. He chose his redeemed from
the world He chooses among them to peculiar positions and to eminent honors. Our Lord
certainly promised that his apostles should be
exalted "to a distinction corresponding with the
services they have rendered" Matt. xix. 28. He
assured them "that in the future glory their place
would correspond with their services in their high
office." His call of them while on earth to their
ministry was, as men would say, arbitrary, and
through that they were exalted to a pre-eminent
honor and rank in heaven. And surely if the
differences in nature and in grace which God himself makes here are right, they cannot be wrong
there

It is not to be doubted that between the divine
choice and human capacities there is a close connection. But, after all, back of everything is the
energy of God. His sovereign choice cannot be

destroyed.   Over and above the natural and
gracious development to which I have already
referred as itself working out the gradations of
heaven, we cannot deny that he may there,
according to his good pleasure, select from
among the glorified for special honors and special
works.   In this we find a thought of peculiar
comfort.   Everywhere we meet with those who
are beaten down by the adverse circumstances of
their position; persons of peculiar piety and rare
excellence whose opportunities do not help them;
persons of sensitive faithfulness, but little worldly
wisdom; or persons cut down by death before
their natural and gracious powers have commenced to be fruitful.   As we see society here,
it exhibits unjust and great inequalities   But
God seeth not as man seeth.   We doubt not
that in the land of perfect bliss that class of the
redeemed who have attracted but little of the
attention of the world and of the Church, who
have indeed rather been looked down upon, but
whose lives have had a peculiarly spiritual flavor,
will be found exalted by the sovereign grace of
God to positions of the highest rank, greatest
brilliancy, heaviest responsibility and widest activity in the fields of eternal usefulness.

AS THE STARS.

2. The prophet Daniel declares (xii. 2, 3), "Many of them that sleep in the dust of the earth shall awake, some to everlasting life, and some to shame and everlasting contempt. And they that be wise shall shine as the brightness of the firmament; * and they that turn many to righteousness, as the stars for ever and ever." This refers to the condition of those who are to enjoy everlasting life after the general resurrection. Our

* Archbishop Leighton has a quaint remark (toward the close of his fourth sermon) for the encouragement of humble Christians who have no great and distinct light to throw upon the world: " There is a certain company of small stars in the firmament which, though they cannot be each one severally seen, yet, being many, their united light makes a conspicuous brightness in the heavens, which is called the *Milky Way;* so, though the shining of every private Christian is not so much severally remarkable, yet the concourse and meeting of their light together will make a bright path of holiness shine in the Church " But, in addition, let it be remembered that God's eye resolves the nebulæ into distinct stars, as do our telescopes of increasing power, and that those which are only indistinct haziness to the naked eye are really far larger and brighter than our planets, which appear to us so prominent So in the kingdom of God. God sees some of the largest and brightest souls whose glory the world does not discern, whom the Church does not specially honor. The least here, the greatest above

Saviour, in Matt. xiii. 43, speaking of all the blessed, says, "Then shall the righteous shine forth as the sun in the kingdom of their Father." But he is there simply contrasting the happy position of the righteous with the miserable condition of the wicked, and, compared with the gloomy darkness of the lost world, the lowest position in heaven is as the shining of the sun compared with the dark and charred embers on which a smouldering fire has passed. The prophecy of Daniel, however, compares the glory of some of the saved in heaven with that of others. In the second verse he presents the great contrast between the righteous and the wicked, when he says that the former shall awake to everlasting life, the latter to shame and everlasting contempt. But in the third verse, speaking of the righteous, all of whom, as wise, shall shine as the brightness of the firmament, he asserts that some "who were honored above others in their usefulness here," by fruitful labors in his cause for the conversion of souls, shall have "peculiar degrees of glory conferred upon them hereafter." * Among them there shall be differences as there are among the stars, which shine forth with their varied

* Ridgeley's *Divinity,* ii 295.

degrees of brightness in the one all-pervading glory of the firmament.

What a stimulus this is to active efforts for the good of souls! How encouraging and sustaining to the pastor whose efforts God blesses to the conversion of sinners! What a well-spring of pleasure in the heart it is to feel that there are those to whom he can say as Paul said to the Thessalonians, "Ye are my glory and joy"! 1 Thess. ii. 20. How unutterably thrilling to know that they shall appear in his crown of rejoicing in that day when the Lord shall make up his jewels!

Nor is it only the pastor and the preacher who may enjoy this blessedness. There have been poor and unlearned men and women on whom the rich and the high-born looked with contempt, but whom God has abundantly favored in this way. There is not a Christian who may not attain to some degree of that future glory. Reader, the Master calls you to it. Strive with the power of God, by your prayers, your words, your life, to turn some unto righteousness. If you do not, should you get to heaven yourself, you will indeed reflect the brightness of that Sun which makes the spiritual firmament resplendent with its glory;

18

but you shall be like one of the little stars that
we can just see and no more.

It may be that the prophetic declaration of
Daniel, under the guidance of the Holy Spirit,
suggested to Paul one of the richest sentences in
that chapter which, amid all the divinely beautiful
portions of the Bible, has ever appeared to me
among the most magnificent and soul-stirring.
In the unanswerable logic of its reasoning, based
as well upon facts as upon principles; its conclusive sweeping away of objections; the grandeur
of its rhetoric; the force and beauty of its figures;
the gorgeousness of its imagination; the height
of its eloquence, unfalteringly sustained to the
end; the power with which it touches the inmost
affections of the soul; and the clarion ring of
triumph with which it closes,—the fifteenth chapter of the First Epistle to the Corinthians stands
in the highest place of literature, ancient and
modern.   No speech, no writing, that equals it
can be found.   I can never peruse it without emotion.   My soul is ever borne captive along on its
grand argument.   If anything could on earth
introduce me to the ecstatic vision of heaven, I
believe it is that chapter.   I have sometimes
thought that if I were placed in a position in

which I could retain but one leaf of the Bible, I would keep that. Certainly when I come to die I could desire nothing better than to be able, with a strong faith, to utter its glorious conclusion, " O death! where is thy sting? O grave! where is thy victory? The sting of death is sin; and the strength of sin is the law. But thanks be to God, which giveth us the victory through our Lord Jesus Christ!"

But the particular sentence in it which bears on the point that I am now presenting is contained in the forty-first and forty-second verses: " There is one glory of the sun, and another glory of the moon, and another glory of the stars; for one star differeth from another star in glory: so also is the resurrection of the dead." The apostle is showing the absurdity of the objection to the resurrection which is founded on the assumption that the body if raised hereafter must be precisely and atomically what it is here. He overwhelms that objection by referring to the immense varieties of matter that surround us. " Standing as we do in the midst of this wonderful universe, in which we see matter in every conceivable modification, from a clod of earth to a sunbeam, from dust to the lustre of the human eye, how unutter-

ably absurd it is to say that if we are to have
bodies hereafter, they must be as gross and heavy
and as corruptible as those which we now have!"
He shows, therefore, that the raised form may be
a body, and yet differ as much from what it is now
as the light of the sun differs from a piece of
clay. "As the heavenly bodies differ from the
earthly bodies, and as one star differs from another
star, so the resurrection body will differ from our
present body." *   But under this great idea, and
as one of its manifestations, he implies the different glories of the saints in the resurrection. All
the heavenly luminaries have a glory superior to
terrestrial bodies, but when compared together
some are more glorious than others.   In like
manner, "the glory of the least saint in heaven is
inconceivably greater than that of the greatest on
earth. The glory indeed is full and complete in
its kind; yet when compared with the glory of
others it may in some circumstances fall short of
it;" † just as when we go out on a starlight night
we find various shades of brightness, from the
clear silvery light of Venus as she moves conspicuous in the foreground of heaven to the almost

* Hodge on 1 Corinthians xv. 41, 42.

† Ridgeley, ii. 295.

imperceptible twinkling of the fixed star that
seems to shrink from view.

3. In the twenty-fifth chapter of the Gospel
according to Matthew our Lord teaches the
principles on which the awards of the judgment
day are to be made. The two parables which it
contains, in connection with the similar one in
Luke xix. 12–27, bear particularly on the question that I am considering They illustrate the
condition of the Church on earth,˙Christ's bodily
absence from it since his ascension, and his coming to it again in judgment. One idea running
through them is that the visible organization
will, to the end, be composed of two classes, true
and false professors God knows that better than
the world does, though men are foolishly fond of
excusing themselves and attacking the cause of
Christ on account of it.

The parable of the Virgins enforces the duty
of watchfulness and warns against declension
from Christian faithfulness. The true professors
who are prepared for the coming of the Lord
enter in to the eternal marriage with the Church.
The others, who have the lamp of profession with-

out the oil of grace, the form of godliness without the power, are taken unawares. In tribulation they seek for the oil when it is too late, and are for ever shut out from the feast.

The parable of the Talents * has an additional idea. It shows not merely the duty of watching for the coming of the Lord, but also that " of active service in Christ's cause, and the reward that awaits the faithful as well as the doom that must come upon unfaithfulness." The Lord trav-

---

* Macaulay (*Life and Letters*, 1. 192) tells a story of the celebrated Lady Holland which gives a little bit of history of the word "talents," while it is also humiliatingly suggestive of ignorance in high life : " We talked about the word *talents* and its history. I said that it had first appeared in theological writing, that it was a metaphor taken from the parable in the New Testament, and that it had gradually passed from the vocabulary of divinity into common use. I challenged her to find it in any classical writer on general subjects before the Restoration, or even before the year 1700. I believe that I might safely have gone down later. She seemed surprised by this theory, never having, so far as I could judge, heard of the parable of the Talents. I did not tell her, though I might have done so, that a person who professes to be a critic in the delicacies of the English language ought to have the Bible at his fingers' ends." Lady Holland's ignorance, I suspect, could be almost paralleled among our public characters. It is not safe for ministers to assume too accurate a knowledge by the people generally of the facts and phraseology of the Scriptures.

els into a far country. To every one of his servants he gives a talent or talents to be used in his
cause. The unprofitable servant is punished for his
neglect to use his talent. Those to whom two
and five talents are committed, and who employ
them for the Lord, receive their reward accordingly.

This parable, it is true, does not bring promi-
nently forward the differences in the degree of the
reward to the different persons. But now turn to
the very similar narrative in Luke xix. 12–27.
The Lord compares himself to a nobleman receiving a kingdom, and giving to his servants
authority over cities in return for their faithful
use of what he had committed to them in his
absence. The good servant who by use had
increased fivefold the pound bestowed upon him
is rewarded with the authority over five cities;
the other good servant, who had been even more
faithful in the use of his pound and had multiplied
it tenfold, receives—only as much as the other?
No, but ten cities. If the parable teaches anything, it plainly proves that the heavenly rewards
are in proportion to the useful employment of
that which God has bestowed.*

* ' It is not for the one pound given, but for the ten which he
had gained, hat the reward is given. This implies degrees of

It may occur to some that the parable of the
Vineyard Laborers (Matt. xx. 1–16) seems to
teach a doctrine different from this. The man
who works .therein but one hour receives as
much as those who bear the burden and heat of
the day. A careful examination, however, shows
that the purpose which Jesus had in view in
uttering that discourse was a very different one.
It was called forth by the mercenary question
of Peter in the preceding chapter: "Behold, we
have forsaken all and followed thee; what shall
we have therefore?"* And it is designed to
illustrate the last verse of that chapter: "Many
that are first shall be last; and the last shall be

rewards A city is the reward for each pound gained, and yet
not even a cottage (much less a city) could be purchased for a
pound. Great is the grandeur and variety of things in the
kingdom of God, although they are not yet known to us."—
Bengel on Luke xix 17

* Even Brahmanism condemns that. "The highest of all
virtues is disinterested goodness, performed from the love of
God and based on the knowledge of the Veda. A religious
action, performed from hope of reward in this world or the next,
will give one a place in the lowest heaven. But he who per-
forms good actions without hope of reward, perceiving the
supreme Soul in all beings, and all beings in the supreme Soul,
fixing his mind on God, approaches the divine nature."—
Clarke's *Ten Religions*, p. 113.

first." It was exceedingly difficult to impress clear views of the nature of Christ's kingdom upon the minds of the apostles. They never did receive them during his sojourn on earth. From the erroneous notions which they held flowed the question of Peter, who seems to have been antici- pating earthly distinctions. The spirit in which he put his question also was wrong, inasmuch as it seemed to breathe a claim for their good deeds, as though they deserved the reward at Christ's hands The grand underlying idea of the para- ble, therefore, is that God as a sovereign can do as he pleases with his own; and so long as any are dealt with on the principles of pure justice, and receive all that has been promised to them, they have no right to complain if in the exercise of his sovereignty he should treat others more liberally. It condemns all claim of right on the part of any, for whatsoever is received is still a free gift. It discountenances the habit of "looking for rewards prematurely and wrongfully; making invidious comparisons and claims ; having an envious eye to others' pay; and the disposition to act so lit- tle on the high principles of individual duty." Moreover, some who enter late in life into the Church of God and its work do more than

others who commenced earlier. On fire with
zeal and energy, they accomplish greater results
in months than other and more sluggish natures
do in years. The last are thus first.

A difference in the framework of the two
parables of the Talents and the Pounds reveals
another important element on which the judgment
of God is based. " In the Talents each servant
receives a different number of them—five, two,
one; in the Pounds all receive the same—one
pound; also in the Talents each of the faithful
servants shows the *same* fidelity by doubling what
he received—the five are made ten, the two four;
in the Pounds, each, receiving the same, renders
a *different* return—one making his pound ten,
another five. Plainly, therefore, the intended lesson is different—the one illustrating *equal fidelity
with different degree of advantage;* the other,
*different degrees of improvement of the same oppor-
tunities."* * " And thus it is that the most exalted

* " If the different number of *talents* in the latter parable
represents different spheres of labor, greater or less, corresponding to different measures of power, then the one *pound* in the
former must represent the *one* common endowment of Christians
—the one divine life or the one divine truth received into the
life in all believers—the one divine power, proving itself by its
fruits in all who partake of it, but yet admitting of different

in intellectual gifts or wealth or opportunity—
though consecrating all these in beautiful fidelity
to Christ—may be found occupying no higher
position in the kingdom above than the lowest in
all these respects who have shown equal fidelity
to the common Master " *   Some with fewer talents, but greater faithfulness in the use of them,
may do more with their little, and therefore
realize more for God and themselves, than others
who are more favored in natural gifts and opportunities, but less zealous in their use.   "Unto
whomsoever much is given, of him shall be much
required." Luke xii. 48.   God in his rewards has
regard to the different powers with which he
endowed his people, to the opportunities with
which they were favored, to the fidelity with
which they employed both ; and, under the com-
pound interest of Heaven's bank, superior fidelity
may repay some of the least favored in natural
and gracious gifts and opportunities on earth with
the highest returns hereafter.†

degrees of fruitfulness according to the completeness with which
it is willingly received and appropriated."—Neander's *Life of
Christ*.

 * Brown on Luke xix and Matt. xxv.

 † Bengel's comment on the word " occupy " in Luke xix. 13 is :
" πραγματενσασθε, *trade* with this   This commandment accords

Dr. Hanna in his graceful *Life of Christ* brings out another important idea: " In the curiously modified structure of these two parables, by that wherein they agree and that wherein they differ, how strikingly is the double lesson taught that while each man's proper and direct reward shall exactly tally with his proper and individual work, yet that in the distribution of extra or additional favors regard shall be had to existing position, existing possessions, existing capability —that the awards of heaven shall be adjusted in duplicate proportion to the service previously rendered and to the capacity presently possessed !"

The training and use of the capacities and powers with which we have been favored is itself a happiness here. In the degree to which our talents have thus been educated we shall, when summoned by death, enter the glorious land. The higher the progress that we have thus made, the more exalted shall be the position from which we will start upon the perfectly purified and spiritualized eternal activities of heaven; and those activities, the very exercise of our capacities, will

in sense with that noted one, *be good bankers* (make the most of your money)."

be a joy. Thus the education of earth trains us for action in heaven adapted to its character, and returns through eternity its reward upon itself.

"In short, the happiness of each individual will be exactly apportioned to his susceptibility of happiness Great and various as may be his capacity or susceptibility for the enjoyment of happiness, just so great and various will his happiness certainly be hereafter." * As an important element in the bliss of the glorified is "constant increase in knowledge and in the useful exercise of all their powers," † the amount of knowledge possessed at their entrance upon the celestial world, and the powers they developed here, and the extent to which they cultivated them, form important factors in their capabilities of joy. "The outward circumstances of their being will be such as to minister to their increasing blessedness." ‡ God has for them fields of work, activity in which will be its own happiness. Therefore the powers trained by use here fit for, and help to measure, the joy of the hereafter.

This thought invests our *habitual* life on earth

---

* Knapp's *Theology*, p. 559
† Hodge's *Theology*, iii. 861. ‡ Ibid.

with a far-reaching practical importance * It also
draws the sting from one of the mysterious provi-
dences of God. " How many men are born with
intellectual faculties and powers which they can
never fully develop here, either because they die
early or are wholly destitute of the means and
opportunities for development and cultivation!" †
How many, when just ready for active life after
years of study, are cut down by death ! Is their
preparation lost? Nay, they are only removed to
some broader field, in which their development
continues and every talent yields its profit to the
great Giver of all.

If any, observing the different ranks which
exist in this world, the varieties of talents which

* Neander's remarks on the *one*-talent and the *one*-pound servant should warn the falsely humble: " One only is wholly
rejected—he that guards carefully the sum committed to him and
loses nothing, but *gains* nothing. . . . He represents those whose
mistaken apprehensions of the account they will have to render
keep them in inactivity, and *who retire from the active labors of
the world in order to avoid contamination from its unholy atmosphere,* . . those who, with inferior powers, have insufficient
confidence, and make the smallness of their gifts and the narrowness of their sphere of labor a plea for inactivity; such as
say, comparing their talents and opportunities with those of
others, ' What can be expected of me, to whom so little has been
given ?' '   † Knapp, 556.

are possessed, the modes in which some of the least spiritual and lovely seem to be most highly favored, be inclined to murmur at the inequality, let it be remembered that some of the apparently highest and most prominent of earth do the least for God ; that spiritual talents weigh more in the balances of heaven than the merely mental, social and political ; that suffering and sympathy sometimes do a greater work than the most widely-trumpeted achievements ; that

> "One flash of light which genius can impart,
> One grand conception in a wise man's head,
> One gentle movement of a loving heart,
> Or tear for woe of others kindly shed,
> Is worth ten thousand times such meaner things
> As rank of princes and the pomp of kings;"

and that the divine awards will be adjusted in the light of this.

It is one of the pleasant conceits of Kurtz* that "if man had been obedient to his divine destiny, and in his state of innocence peopled this planet to its utmost bounds, his mission might have been extended to those neighboring worlds which are so closely related to ours, so as to draw them also within the circle of his activity, and

* *History of the Old Covenant,* i. lxxxii.

thus to lead them toward that perfection for
which they were destined.   In the course of his
development he might perhaps have acquired new
powers by which to pass from world to world, as
now he passess from shore to shore."   If so, the
boldest flight of imagination cannot reach to the
avenues of activity which may be opened up in
the glorified future for the spiritual powers that
are trained here.   For, "however incomprehensi-
ble and exalted the terms in which the New Testament describes the blessedness of the redeemed,
they imply nothing alien to or different from
man's original destiny.   The glory of his original
state and that of his state of perfectness are
related as germ and development, as destiny and
realization." *

* Dr. Storrs, in his " Aim of Christianity for those who accept
it " (*Biblical Repertory*, xxxix. 382), speaking of the expression
" that ye might be filled unto all the fullness of God," grandly
says : " We cannot tell—thank God, as yet, in this infancy of
our being, we *cannot* tell !—what that shall be.   But we know
that when it is realized by us, realized in us, then the universe,
in all the untrodden ways which science itself has not explored,
becomes but our familiar home   Then that ascension of Christ
our Lord, in which he paced the liquid air as if it were a sapphire floor, does but prophesy ours.   And then the unshadowed
effulgence of heaven is only the atmosphere for which we were
through him new born."

Isaac Taylor, with a use of his imagination which is not lawless, but founded upon a scientific fact, says: "Might we rest for a moment upon an animating conception (aided by the actual analogy of light) such as this—namely, that the field of the visible universe is the theatre of a vast social economy, holding rational intercourse at great distances? Let us claim leave to indulge a while the belief, when we contemplate the starry heavens, that speech, inquiry and response, commands and petitions, debate and instruction, are passing to and fro; nor need it be denied to us to imagine the pealing anthem of praise at stated seasons arising from worshipers in all quarters, and flowing on, like the noise of many waters, until it reach the courts of the central heavens." *

Still further, as connected with the development and use of our talents here, he makes this suggestion—I think wisely: "The power of actually traversing the fields of the material universe we may, with some show of reason, anticipate as intended for a being to whom already so much has been granted . We may readily conceive of a state of things in which there may be services to be performed, enterprises to be undertaken

* *Physical Theory of Another Life*, p. 193, 194.

19

and a promotion to be aimed at, such as none but
the bold and the strong shall be equal to, and
none but the aspiring shall dare to attempt.
These services may . . . demand sudden exertions
of intelligence and a ready recurrence to resources under circumstances that would amaze
and baffle all but the calmly courageous. Moreover, there may be high advantages to be
snatched by the few whose flight can be long
sustained and is the most steady; there may be
dominations to be exercised which those shall
secure to themselves who can prove, by service
done, that they are equal to the weight of the
sceptre It is surely a frivolous notion (if any
actually entertain it) that the vast and intricate
machinery of the universe and the profound
scheme of God's government are now soon to
reach a resting-place, where nothing more shall
remain to active spirits through an eternity but
recollections of labor, anthems of praise and
inert repose. . . . All the practical skill we ac-
quire in managing affairs, all the versatility, the
sagacity, the calculation of chances, the patience
and assiduity, the promptitude and facility, as
well as the higher virtues which we are learning
every day, may well find scope in a world such

as is rationally anticipated when we think of heaven as the stage of life that is next to follow the discipline of earth." *

The pre-eminently scriptural and spiritual Baxter, giving reasons why it is far better to be with Christ in the glorious land than to continue here, says : " There are good works in heaven, and far more and better than on earth. There will be more life and power for action ; more love to God and one another to excite to action; more likeness to God and Christ in doing good, as well as being good; more union with the beneficent Jesus, to make us also beneficent; and more communion, by each contributing to the welfare of the whole and sharing in their common returns to God." And he adds: " Probably God makes glorified spirits the agents of his beneficence to inferior creatures." †

Therefore, the daily training of the powers which God has bestowed upon us is preparing us for our position in heaven in relation to God and to each other, and for the peculiar fields in which we will be active in the great republic of the universe.

---

* *Physical Theory*, pp. 106, 157–159.
† *Dying Thoughts*, ch 4.

"THE THINGS DONE IN THE BODY."

4. The next passage to which I refer presents
in a very striking manner the connection that
exists between our acts here and their rewards
hereafter: "For we must all appear before the
judgment seat of Christ; that every one may
receive the things done in his body, according to
that he hath done, whether it be good or bad."
2 Cor. v. 10.

"That every one may *receive the things done
in his body.*" Our acts are investments laid up
for the future, and we are to *receive* them *back*,
for that is the force of the word in the original
Greek. The figure is very forceful. When men
invest a sum of money for a certain length of
time, they expect on the day of payment to
receive back the full amount of their investment. Those who invest more than others
receive back more than others. Our lives are
lives of investment for the future. Day by day,
hour by hour, through our affections, our
thoughts, our words, our acts, we are adding
to the sum; and at the judgment day the accounts shall all be settled, and we shall receive
back what we have deposited in God's eternal

treasury. Herein may be a hundred-fold gain for the life to come.

I scarcely know a verse in the Bible that should be more startling to unforgiven sinners, and more stirring in its exhortations to penitent believers.

Impenitent reader, consider how grievously you sin against yourself by continuing in your Christless state. You are laying up no blessed investments for the future. You are, on the contrary, storing up treasures of wrath. Many of your past acts may have dropped out of your recollection, but they are laid up against the final account. Taking only the sins which you may remember, how will you meet them at the awful day? If, before death comes upon you, you should through the tender mercy of our God trust in the crucified Lamb for salvation, you shall be forgiven. The atoning blood will wipe -out the record of past guilt. But if you delay, how little time may be allowed you to lay up other heavenly treasures! Every impenitent hour decreases the amount which you might otherwise have. Hasten to commence the blessed investment

You too, believer, are laying up an investment.

Every sin that you commit takes away from, every good deed for Christ's sake adds to, that investment. Be therefore encouraged the more to resist temptation and constantly to work for Jesus. Not even the drop of cold water, given to a disciple in the name of a disciple, shall be found wanting in the heavenly reservoir from which you will for ever drink. The kindly deeds that you may cease to recollect in the struggles and the progress of your daily course, which crowd new occasions of usefulness upon you, will hereafter reappear in very precious forms. Pre-eminently shall such "works follow" you. Rev. xiv. 13.

REAPING AS IS SOWN.

5. The foregoing passage manifestly contains a principle which teaches a difference in the rewards of the future life. The only other one that I shall refer to presents the same idea in a somewhat different, and perhaps even more forcible, shape.

"Be not deceived, God is not mocked; for whatsoever a man soweth, that shall he also reap For he that soweth to the flesh shall of the flesh reap corruption ; but he that soweth to the Spirit

shall of the Spirit reap life everlasting." Gal. vi.
7, 8. And "he which soweth sparingly shall reap
also sparingly; and he which soweth bountifully
shall reap also bountifully." 2 Cor. ix. 6.

At the harvest-time the farmer expects to reap
the same kind of grain that he has sown. One
who sows a noxious seed will get a noxious crop.
One who sows wheat expects wheat in return.
But he also expects to reap a far greater quantity
than he had sown. The crop he expects to be in
proportion to the seed. He who sows most has,
other things being equal, the largest harvest.

The application of this is evident, but the extent of its operation must be such as no human
imagination can picture The comparisons, of
the death and burial of the body and of the acts of
our daily life, to the sowing of seed, are suggestive of a most wonderful changing and increasing
production all through eternity. Look at a single
grain of wheat as it is placed in the ground; then
observe its transformation as it grows, and the
large number of grains which appear from it in
the harvest; and remember that every act in time
is a seed planted for eternity, each to grow up, not
merely into the same or a similar grain, but into
an innumerable crop, and to go on for ever devel-

oping itself. It is infinitely self-multiplying. Therefore increase the good deeds of life, that you may have an infinite multiplication of them and of their joys in the world to come;

> " Rouse to some work of high and holy love,
>   And thou an angel's happiness shalt know,
>   Shalt bless the earth while in the world above;
>   The good begun by thee shall onward flow
>   In many a branching stream, and wider grow;
>   The seed that, in these few and fleeting hours,
>   Thy hands unsparing and unwearied sow,
>   Shall deck thy grave with amaranthine flowers,
>   And yield thee fruits divine in heaven's immortal bowers."

If it may be, keep on in your earnest work until the very last hour of earth. Let death find you intent upon it. Not only will that give you the more abundant entrance into the glorious kingdom, and introduce you on the other side of the river into its blissful rewards with the greater rapture, but it will divest the mighty change of all the gloom which rests upon this side of it; for " he that dies in an earnest pursuit is like one that is wounded in hot blood, who, for the time, scarce feels the hurt; and therefore a mind fixed and bent upon somewhat that is good doth avert the dolors of death." *

* Bacon's Essay, *Of Death.*

These, then, seem to be the facts which are established by the inspired word: God's election of the redeemed unto eternal life extends, in the distribution of its blessings and the apportionment of positions for work, through eternity and into heaven; and sinless differences, such as exist in grace, may be looked for in glory. In this will be found a remedy for the many unjust discriminations which are found in this stage of our existence. It will award honors and labors properly, according to the real desert and ability of the glorified. The varied capacities and tendencies with which souls are born into the world, as developed, trained, exercised here, largely decide their positions, lines of activity and shades of joy in the future. The daily deeds of this life will themselves be treasures of varied bliss in memory and in the mutual associations that they will make among the inhabitants of the happy land. Moreover, those acts will be eternally productive and reproductive of other acts and other joys. We are seed-sowing; and the seed now planted will hereafter be reaped, and sown and reaped on for ever and ever.

All these facts are suggestive of immense differences in happiness, in position, in glory in God's

eternal home; and they invest our daily education and our daily conduct with the most transcendent importance—an importance which is made
infinite by the consideration that the development
for the various degrees of the endless and ever-
expanding glory must commence this side of
physical death.   At the temporary separation of
soul and body is pronounced the sentence, "He
that is unjust, let him be unjust still; and he
which is filthy, let him be filthy still; and he that
is righteous, let him be righteous still; and he
that is holy, let him be holy still." Rev. xxii. 11.
"There are opportunities for work now given
which if not used here can never recur in the
world to come."   Therefore, "whatsoever thy hand
findeth to do, do it with thy might; for there is
no work, nor device, nor knowledge, nor wisdom, in the grave, whither thou goest." Eccles.
ix 10.

In the light of the declarations of Scripture
that have thus been examined we are prepared
for a few considerations which in themselves
would not be conclusive, but which are founded
upon principles of human nature that are con-
sonant with the written revelation of God's
will.

The analogy of the present life gives support
to this view. That the people of God enjoy
various degrees of blessedness here is undoubted.
These differences do not depend altogether upon
the degree of sanctification which they have
experienced. No doubt they have a very intimate connection with this. Other things being
equal, the more a believer is purified the greater
will be his happiness. I would not, however,
found upon this fact an argument in regard to
the future state, because at death the souls of all
believers are made perfectly holy. But the
measure of enjoyment which men possess is, to
a very considerable extent, determined by the
faculties and capacities that God has conferred
upon them. These faculties and capacities are
not in power alike in all at the beginning.
Minds are not equal originally. There are some
that can scarcely be raised above the clod of
earth on which we tread. They either cannot or
will not be trained to think Education is dis-
tasteful to them. Others as soon as they open
upon the world around them spring into activity,
eagerly seek for information, and, with an almost

instantaneous bound, commence to ascend the ladder of knowledge. At the commencement there are thus differences in the power of enjoyment which lies potentially in the mental faculties.

Further, there are differences caused by the improvement and use which men make of their minds. The acquisition of knowledge is one of the richest sources of happiness. There is a pleasure in the mere act of acquisition,* as well as in contemplating what we have acquired. The man who has stored his mind with a fund of knowledge, and is able to make widely-extended excursions through the domain of God's works and word, has in himself a richer perennial fountain than is possessed by the mental sluggard who lets his talent run to waste. The mind of an astronomer like Newton, who could soar at will through the vast expanse of heaven, and with his measuring-line nicely adjust the distances of the stars, and in his balances accurately weigh the influence that one has upon another—who saw the sun to be the centre of our system, around which the earth, the moon and the

* The philosophic reader will recollect the perilous extreme to which Sir William Hamilton pushes this principle in his *Metaphysics*, Lecture I.

planets revolve—and who could pierce into other systems, all revolving round the great centre of the universe, the throne of God,—had the means of greater enjoyment than were possessed by the peasant who regarded the sun as a huge ball of fire, and imagined he heard the seething of the ocean which in the evening received the burning mass into its bosom. The philosopher, again, who explores the secrets of his own mind has the same advantage over the witless man who never stops to look within. The study of the works of God is a great source of pleasure. The more thorough the study and the greater the acquisition, when made in the right spirit, the greater the means of happiness.

This is also true in regard to the study of the word of God. Those who, in the use of the faculties that God has bestowed upon them, seek in it for knowledge as for silver, and search for it as for hid treasures—whose great delight it is to look into the mystery of redemption and learn the ways of God to man—and who, in the exploration have their faith in Christ and all Christian graces deepened,—have a source of happiness which the neglecter or merely formal reader of the Bible knows nothing of. It is one which all

readers may possess in great degree. They may
not be able to explore the vast labyrinth of scientific knowledge through which the highly educated mind may roam, but they can study God's
book. To the extent to which they neglect it,
they depreciate their stock of enjoyment here, and
to the same extent they incapacitate themselves
for the higher degrees of blessedness hereafter.

For unless we suppose that at death the souls
of believers are not merely made perfect in holiness, but that some other change, for which we
have no scriptural authority, is made in their constitution and furniture, we are warranted in con-
cluding that differences similar to these may exist
in the future. The existence of the soul hereafter is the unbroken continuance of its life here.
It enters upon the hereafter with the character it
has acquired here, and with its capacities and
faculties in the standing to which they have been
educated   We have no ground for supposing
that any of its powers are taken from it in the
translation to the other world, or that any other
radical change is made in it than its perfect deliverance from sin and from the effects of sin.*   If

* It is worth while to quote (in their union, which modifies the
influence of each) two of the fundamental principles that Bishop

this be so, it is evident that the higher the degree
to which at death it has been educated in the use

Butler lays down in the beginning of his *Analogy*, observing the
way in which he bases them on the great principle that skeptical
scientists try to turn against our religion: " 1. From our being
born into the present world in the helpless, imperfect state of
infancy, and having arrived from thence to mature age, we find
it to be a general law of nature in our own species that the same
creatures, the same individuals, should exist in different degrees
of life and perception, with capacities of action, of enjoyment
and suffering in one period of their being greatly different from
those appointed them in another period of it. . . . But the
states of life in which we ourselves existed formerly, in the
womb and in our infancy, are almost as different from our present in mature age as it is possible to conceive any two states or
degrees of life can be. Therefore, that we are to exist hereafter
in a state as different (suppose) from our present as this is from
our former, is but according to the analogy of nature—according
to a natural order or appointment of the very same kind with
what we have already experienced. 2. We know we are endued
with capacities of action, of happiness and misery, for we are
conscious of acting, of enjoying pleasure and suffering pain.
Now, that we have these powers and capacities before death is a
presumption that we shall retain them through and after death;
indeed, a probability of it abundantly sufficient to act upon,
unless there be some positive reason to think that death is the
destruction of those living powers; because there is in every
case a probability that all things will continue as we experience
they are in all respects, except those in which we have some
reason to think they will be altered. This is that kind of pre-

of the means which the Spirit of God blesses, the
more thoroughly prepared it is for those measures
of happiness which are connected with the use of
its faculties.

It is very probable that in heaven the souls of
the redeemed make new and ever new advances
in the knowledge of God and his ways, for if
they could ever thoroughly know God they would
be gods themselves.   It is probable "that the
understanding of glorified saints shall receive
very considerable improvement from those objects
which shall be presented to them, and from the
perpetual discoveries which will be made of the
glorious mysteries of divine grace, whereby the
whole scene of providence and its subserviency
to their eternal happiness shall be opened to raise
their wonder and enhance their praise.   As it is
not inconsistent with the perfect blessedness of
the angels to desire to know more of this mystery which they are said to look into, and as their
joy is increased by those new occasions which

sumption or probability from analogy expressed in the very
word *continuance*, which seems our only natural reason for
believing the course of the world will continue to-morrow as it
has done so far as our experience or knowledge of history can
carry us back."

daily present themselves, why may not the same be said with respect to the saints in heaven, especially if we consider that this will redound so much to the glory of God, as well as give us more raised ideas of that happiness which they shall be possessed of?" *

THE NATURE OF THE HEAVENLY BLESSEDNESS.

A further confirmation of the truth that I am exhibiting is found in the nature of the heavenly blessedness.

Perhaps there is scarcely any point on which popular notions are so vague as on this. Very few Christians, comparatively, can give any clear idea of what they mean by the bliss of the future life. The general view is that the everlasting home of the saved is a place of perfect holiness and happiness, and that perfection excludes degrees. But it must be remembered that perfection is a relative term. The perfection of God is very different from the perfection of man. The capacities of men vary: what fills the mind of one may not meet the capabilities of another. You may take a great number of vessels of dif-

* Ridgeley, ii. 296.

ferent sizes and fill them all to overflowing,* and
they will all be perfectly full; but there will be
great differences in the amount which each holds.
The souls of the blessed enter heaven with different capacities. Each is perfectly full of happiness.
Each holds as much as it can contain. But there
are immense varieties of capacity among them.

There is also an indistinctness in the popular
mind as to the source of the happiness of heaven.
It is thought of as something—we know not what
—bestowed from without by God. No doubt there
may be elements in that blessedness of which we
have no idea here. But it must be borne in mind
that "the Scriptures abundantly teach that the
blessedness of heaven is the same for substance

* "It is but little we can receive here—some drops of joy that
enter into *us*—but there *we* shall enter into joy, as vessels put into
a sea of happiness."—*Archbishop Leighton.* That ecstatic joy
of the Lord shall perfectly fill all the souls who enter into it;
but how different the sizes (if I may use a physical expression)
of souls!—of Paul, for instance, and the converted thief, of an
aged saint who has been working and learning through a protracted course, and an infant! The education and the activities
of a long and zealous life enlarge the capacities for joy. As
Thomas Boston has it in his *Fourfold State:* "As a narrow
vessel cannot contain the ocean, so neither can the finite creature
comprehend the infinite Good; but no measure shall be set to the
enjoyment but what arises from the capacity of the creature."

as that which we now partake of by faith."
Whatever, then, is a fountain of joy in a believing soul here will continue in it hereafter.

One of the rewards which a virtuous and active
mind possesses in this world, and perhaps one of
the purest joys which the soul can possess, is the
knowledge of the good that has been produced
by its example or by its efforts; as one of the
sorest punishments that can be visited upon a
vicious man is the revelation of the fact that his
vices have injured not merely himself, but others
upon whom their influence has passed. Now, of
this there are degrees in this life The more
good that a Christian, through the grace of God,
is enabled to do, the greater the number of opportunities for usefulness that he seizes hold of, the
more consistent his walk, the more heavenly his
example, and the more souls he is instrumental
in leading to Jesus, the deeper is the well-spring
and the more abundant the outgushing of joy
which flows from the grateful knowledge that
God has so blessed him.

Is not the happiest Christian the one who does
most for Jesus in proportion to the talents that
have been committed to him?

Who derives the greatest enjoyment from his

own reflections—the professing Christian who does little more than attend the sanctuary on the Sabbath when it is convenient for him, who spends but little time in religious acts, who finds only a small degree of pleasure in prayer and Christian activity, who, as he looks back upon his life, can see no soul saved through his instrumentality; or his neighbor whose heart burns with love to God, who has prayed for souls in the privacy of his chamber and wrestled with them in conversation, and sought by all the means that he could to lead them to the Saviour of sinners?

The professors of Christ's name who possess not the sweet reflection that they have, under God, been the instrument in turning some souls from darkness to light and from the power of Satan unto the living God, are destitute of one of the purest joys of the Christian life here; and if they enter heaven without it, they shall miss one of the most ravishing elements in its blessedness.

There is nothing in the Bible, nothing in our nature, that leads us to suppose that a believer shall be deprived hereafter of any spiritual source of joy that he now has. On the contrary, he will continue to possess every such pleasure in an intensified degree. As, therefore, this is a fountain of pure and holy joy in this life, it will undoubtedly continue in the future world. Or, as the Redeemer says, "He that reapeth receiveth wages and gathereth fruit unto life eternal: that both he that soweth and he that reapeth may rejoice together." John iv. 36. "Reapers in Christ's harvest receive wages in the enjoyments which accompany their toils in the present life; they gather fruit unto life eternal in the effects of that, contributing to enhance the blessedness of heaven."

Let us, then, rest assured of this: There will be a holy delight in heaven in the recollection of a life spent on earth for Christ; and the longer the life is, and the more thorough our consecration to him in the station in which we are placed, the higher shall be the degree of that delight.

THE DEGREES JUST.

It certainly seems to be but just that these heavenly degrees should exist.

Take the apostle Paul. Follow him through that life of labor and of suffering which he passed in the service of God. Behold him as with burning zeal he treads the scorching sands of Arabia, penetrates the rocky passes of Asia Minor, sails over the tempestuous waters of the Mediterranean, enters into conflict with the philosophers of classic Athens, boldly maintains his ground in the midst of the raging Jewish Sanhedrim, bears testimony for Jesus in heathen Rome and before the emperor. Note the touching catalogue of sufferings which he endured: " In stripes above measure, in prisons more frequent, in deaths oft. Of the Jews five times received I forty stripes save one, thrice was I beaten with rods, once was I stoned, thrice I suffered shipwreck, a night and a day I have been in the deep; in journeyings often, in perils of waters, in perils of robbers, in perils by mine own countrymen, in perils by the heathen, in perils in the city, in perils in the wilderness, in perils in the sea, in perils among false brethren; in weariness and painfulness, in watchings often, in hunger and thirst, in fastings often, in cold and nakedness: besides those things that are without, that which cometh upon me daily, the care of all the churches." 2 Cor. xi. 23–28. See the churches that he established. Read the Epistles which he has left behind, and which are so profitable for doctrine, for reproof, for correction, for instruction

in righteousness. 2 Tim. iii. 16. Count up the
number of souls that the Spirit of God has drawn
to the Saviour through the instrumentality of his
self-denying labors and his writings. Remember
that he had a mind that yet stands peerless among
men, and that it was in his power to have reached
the first rank of his nation; but that he unhesi-
tatingly turned his back upon national advance-
ment, and laid his mind, with all its stores, at the
foot of the cross, determining to make everything
tributary to the preaching of Jesus Christ and
him crucified. Listen to the assured utterance of
his faith as, at the close of his long and eventful
life, with a retrospective glance over what he has
passed through, and the prospective knowledge
of what awaits him, he says, "I have fought a
good fight; I have finished my course, I have
kept the faith. Henceforth there is laid up for
me a crown of righteousness, which the Lord the
righteous Judge shall give me at that day." 2 Tim.
iv. 7, 8. Does it not appear right that he should
occupy a higher rank in the kingdom of glory
than the poor malefactor who, as the light of his
earthly life was about to go out, turned the eye
of faith to Jesus—saved, but not the instrument
of saving others?

There goes a young man who has only to speak
the word and the treasures of literature, the
enjoyments of opulence and the attentions of
friends are freely yielded to him. He might sit
down in a life of intellectual and social enjoyment.
But, rejoicing in the hope of the heavenly inheritance and his heart touched with the love of
Jesus, he enters upon a course of self-denial and
activity. Across the sea he sails to proclaim the
unsearchable riches of Christ to the dying heathen.
He seeks for no earthly reward. He covets no
worldly honor. He indulges in no luxurious
style of living. Burning with zeal, yearning for
the salvation of perishing souls, he scarcely stops,
day or night, the sounding forth of his earnest
entreaties, his soul-stirring appeals, to them to
turn from the error of their way and live. Has
Henry Martyn been rewarded with no higher
position in the kingdom of heaven than has been
assigned to other young men of his class, who, if
Christians in reality, yet gave themselves up very
largely to the social enjoyments of their rank, and
made few efforts for the spread of the Redeemer's
kingdom ?

Look at our various churches. Would it com-
port with our ideas of rectitude to suppose that a

professing Christian of wealth, position and influence, who gives but little of his means toward
the support of the gospel in his own neighborhood and throughout the world, and scarcely
makes an effort to lead a soul to Jesus, shall be as
abundantly blessed as his fellow-member who, in
an equal position, gives liberally and labors zeal-
ously for the cause of religion? Nay; there was
another idea in the mind of Paul when he wrote
to Timothy: "Charge them that are rich in this
world, that they be not high-minded, nor trust in
uncertain riches, but in the living God, who giveth
us richly all things to enjoy: that they do good,
that they be rich in good works, ready to distrib-
ute, willing to communicate; laying up in store
for themselves a good foundation against the time
to come, that they may lay hold on eternal life."
1 Tim. vi. 17–19.

Can we suppose that those of the poor, whether
in money or influence or labor, who make their
inability to do a great deal an excuse for their
refusal to do anything for Jesus, shall stand as
high as others of their class who possess the
spirit of the lowly widow when she offered her
two mites to the treasury of the Lord?

There may be many Christians who shall get

only within the gates of heaven because of their
failure to make use of the opportunities with
which God favors them, and to employ in his
cause the means that he bestows upon them.
When we look upon the two great classes of professors, one of whom appear to do everything
and the other almost nothing in the Church, we
are forced to believe one of two things—either
the latter shall not enter the heavenly city because
they are not Christians at all, or, if the seed of
grace is in their hearts and they enter the glorious
place, they shall occupy far lower positions than
their faithful associates: just saved, and singed
by the fire they have escaped.*

* The expression may to some seem bold. But the apostle
Paul justifies it. Speaking of Christian preachers who in their
instructions mingled errors with the fundamental truths of the
gospel, building upon the right foundation, but mingling the
wood, hay and stubble of the false with the gold, silver and
precious stones of the true, he says (in 1 Cor. iii. 14, 15), " If
any man's work abide which he hath built thereupon, he shall
receive a reward. If any man's work shall be burned, he shall
suffer loss; but he himself shall be saved; yet so as by fire:"
that is, as Dr. Charles Hodge comments, " with difficulty. It is
not enough, therefore, that a minister hold fast to fundamental
truth; he must take heed what he teaches in connection with
that truth. If he mingles with it the wood, hay and stubble of
his own philosophy, he will find himself a loser on the day of

The apostle Peter, in one of the notedly com-
prehensive paragraphs of the Bible, emphasizes
diligence in the development and exercise of the
complete circle of the Christian graces as at once
giving the proof of our salvation, keeping us in
the possession of it, and blessing us with its joys
in rich abundance. Thus he binds together the
three things, so that we cannot be sure of the one
unless we are also securing the others : " According as his divine power hath given unto us all
things that pertain unto life and godliness, through
the knowledge of Him that hath called us to
glory and virtue ; whereby are given unto us exceeding great and precious promises , that by
these ye might be partakers of the divine nature,
having escaped the corruption that is in the
world through lust. And besides this, giving
all diligence, add to your faith, virtue ; and to
virtue, knowledge ; and to knowledge, temperance ;
and to temperance, patience ; and to patience, godliness ; and to godliness, brotherly kindness ; and to

judgment. He will just escape with his life, as a man is rescued
from a burning building. His salvation will not only be effected
with difficulty, but it will be attended with great loss. He will
occupy a lower place in the kingdom of heaven than he would
have done." What a *concio ad clerum* is here !

brotherly kindness, charity. For if these things be in you and abound, they make you that ye shall neither be barren nor unfruitful in the knowledge of our Lord Jesus Christ. But he that lacketh these things is blind, and cannot see afar off, and hath forgotten that he was purged from his old sins. Wherefore the rather, brethren, give diligence to make your calling and election sure; for if ye do these things, ye shall never fall; for so an entrance shall be ministered unto you abundantly into the everlasting kingdom of our Lord and Saviour Jesus Christ." 2 Pet. i. 3–11.

If any truly regenerate person could be so low in his aspirations as to desire merely to be sure of deliverance from perdition and of admission to heaven, the only habit of life which can raise the assurance and guard against apostasy is that diligence which freights the soul with an ever-increasing cargo of spiritual joys, and thereby gives it a rich and triumphant entrance to the heavenly harbor.

Those who commence early in life to be Christians indeed, and day by day cultivate the faculties which God has bestowed upon them, and diligently subsidize the opportunities for usefulness that meet them, are constantly acquiring treasures for heaven and fitting themselves for higher positions of usefulness and joy in the happy land. The longer they live, the greater the wealth which they will carry with them and which shall meet them as they enter the glorious region. Or, if their life here should be cut short before they have succeeded in accomplishing any great results for their Redeemer, their preparation for his work shall not be lost. In the world to which they go they will be active with the spiritual powers which have been developed and cultivated here, and in the world which they leave their influence will continue to gather trophies that shall follow them. In this view the verses of Longfellow contain a great truth:

> " Death takes us by surprise,
>   And stays our hurrying feet ;
> The great design unfinished lies,
>   Our lives are incomplete.
>
> " But in the dark unknown
>   Perfect their circles seem,
> Even as a bridge's arch of stone
>   Is rounded in the stream.
>
> " Alike are life and death
>   When life in death survives,
> And the uninterrupted breath
>   Inspires a thousand lives."

VII:

THE BEAUTY OF HEAVEN: THE ÆSTHETIC LIFE.

HE bewildering beauty of the visions of heaven which have been preserved in the Bible ought to produce an exalted view of the importance of æsthetically cultivating our minds, not only as a part of our daily education for earth, but as a necessary preparation for the highest enjoyment of the world of glory.

When Moses and Aaron, Nadab and Abihu, and seventy of the elders of Israel went up into Mount Horeb, "they saw the God of Israel; and there was under his feet as it were a paved work of a sapphire stone, and as it were the body of heaven in his clearness."* Ex. xxiv. 10.

---

* Or rather, "a work of brilliant sapphire, even like heaven itself for brightness." The Targum of Onkelos has it: "They saw the glory of the God of Israel, and under the throne of his

"A paved work of sapphire," comments Murphy, "is descriptive of a scene of matchless splendor, having the qualities of adamantine solidity, transparency and brilliancy. The substance (or body) of heaven is a phrase for the very heaven itself. Nothing less than the spotless purity and lustre of the skies above is fit to be compared with the inexpressible beauty and grandeur of that which is beneath the feet of the God of Israel."

glory as the work of a precious stone, and as the face of heaven for its clearness." The Jerusalem Targum: "The footstool of his feet as the work of pure sapphire stones, and as the aspect of the heavens when they are cleared from clouds" The Targum of Palestine here affords an instance of what human fancy can do in embellishing God's word: "The glory of the God of Israel; and under the footstool of his feet, which was placed beneath his throne, was like the work of sapphire stone—a memorial of the servitude which the Mizræe had made the children of Israel to serve in clay and bricks (what time) there were women treading clay with their husbands; the delicate young woman with child was also there, and made abortive by being beaten down with the clay. And thereof did Gabriel, descending, make brick, and going up to the heavens on high, set it a footstool under the cathedra of the Lord of the world, whose splendor was as the work of a precious stone, and as the power of the beauty of the heavens when they are clear from clouds" I quote from Etheridge's edition of the Targums, published by the Longmans of London.

In the splendor of that appearance, all the revelations of heaven, especially those which run through the Apocalypse, are bathed. They all suggest more than they express. They raise in our minds the highest expectations, and make us feel that our most vivid conceptions must be unutterably short of the reality.

> " We speak of the realms of the blest,
>   Of that country so bright and so fair,
>   And oft are its glories confessed ;
>   But what must it be *to be there ?*
>
> " We speak of its pathways of gold,
>   Of its walls decked with jewels so rare,
>   Of its wonders and pleasures untold ;
>   But what must it be *to be there ?*"

There are physical and spiritual attractions in this world into the wealth of which only the refined mind can enter. We have no reason to doubt that the same is the case in the Paradise of glorified souls, and shall also be in the reconstructed world of the risen saints.

"The sensitiveness with which many shrink from almost alluding to the physical element of enjoyment in heaven, because it is unworthy to be compared with the spiritual glory that is to be revealed, arises, no doubt, from the half suspicion

21

that there is some necessary connection between materialism and sin; thus forgetting that the body and the outward world which ministers to it are God's handiworks as well as the soul, and that it is he himself who has adjusted their relative workings. And surely it is quite unnecessary to remind you, at any length, how exquisitely God has fashioned our physical frame as the medium of communication with the outer material world. . . . It is true, indeed, that there are grosser appetites of the body which many pervert so as to enslave the spirit, thus abusing by gluttony, drunkenness and every form of sensuality, what God, the merciful and wise, has entrusted to man to be used for wise and merciful ends. But even here there is already perceptible a marked difference between those appetites and the more refined tastes alluded to, inasmuch as the former are found in their abuse to be, strictly speaking, unnatural and destructive of man's happiness; and even in their legitimate use they decay with advancing years, thus proving that the stamp of time is upon them, as on things belonging to a temporary economy; whereas such tastes as enjoy the beautiful in nature or in art, for example, abide in old age with a youthful freshness and more

21

than a youthful niceness of discernment, and so
afford a presumption that they are destined for
immortality.* . . . Who can tell what sources of
refined enjoyment, through the medium of the
spiritual body" (and, I add, for the soul glorified
between the death and resurrection of the body),
"are in store for us in God's great palace of art,
with its endless mansions and endless displays
of glory?   Well may we say of such anticipated
pleasures what good Izaak Walton says of the
singing of birds: 'Lord, if thou hast provided
such music for sinners on earth, what hast thou
in store for thy saints in heaven?'   For if this
little spot of earth is full of scenes of loveliness
to us inexhaustible; if, contemplating these in a
body buoyant with health and strength, we feel it
is a joy even to live and breathe; and if, when seeing God in them all, the expression of praise rises
to the lips, 'Lord, how manifold are thy works!
in wisdom hast thou made them all; the earth is
full of thy riches,'—oh what visions of glory

* Bishop Butler (Pt. i. ch. i. of his *Analogy*) at some length
discusses this principle in a wider form and gives it an extended
application: "There are instances of mortal diseases which do
not at all affect our present intellectual powers; and this affords
a presumption that those diseases" (and death as their culmination) " will not destroy these present powers."

may be spread before the wondering eye throughout the vast extent of the material universe,
comprehending those immense worlds which
twinkle only in the field of the largest telescope
and vanish into the far distance in endless succession, and what sounds may greet the ear from the
as yet unheard music of those spheres! while, for
aught we know, other means of communication
may be opened up to us, with objects ministering
delight to new tastes, and sources of sentient enjoyment discovered which do not exist here or
elude the perception of our present senses." *

THE BEAUTIFUL A PART OF RELIGION.

Therefore, let the great doctrines of grace be
perpetually fed upon as the substantial food of the
soul. Let the peculiarities of the gospel system
form the constant theme of pulpit discourse. Let
faith, repentance, holy living, the duties which are
incumbent on us in the light of God's revealed
word, be continually insisted upon. Let the web
and the woof of preaching to the unconverted be,
" Believe, repent, be converted, be saved;" and to
the believing, " Grow in grace, advance in knowledge, increase in prayer, be zealous in your active

* Dr. Norman Macleod's *Parish Papers*, pp. 101–103

life for the Christ who has redeemed ycu." But let us endeavor not merely to advance ourselves and to help other souls on to heaven, but also to increase the charms of this world. Let us seek to elevate, to refine, to brighten home and social life, knowing that thereby we are also living the life of heaven on earth, and making a better preparation for its manifestation in glory.

The essential connection of this part of our education here with the life hereafter appears from the constitution of the universe and of our minds in their mutual relation. Whatever God has done in the works of his hands we may imitate, and should study and enjoy. Whatever powers he has conferred upon us should be cultivated for this world and the world to come.

GOD THE AUTHOR OF THE BEAUTIFUL.

God is himself the fountain of the beautiful. His works are bathed in the spray which dashes down from his throne and glitters in the light that is reflected from his face.* Heaven is the

---

* "That beauty is founded in God and in the eternal harmony of the divine power was, as is well known, a fundamental idea of Plato, and has frequently been repeated since his days. Supreme beauty is in God   The idea of beauty becomes more perfect the more certainly it can be conceived in harmony with

home of the beautiful, and thence it pours down upon us in a rich perennial stream. The surface of our earth is covered with a gorgeous carpet of God's own weaving, upon which have been placed furniture of the most magnificent description and statuary of the most ravishing expression; while the blue vault of heaven is our fretted roof, and its sparkling orbs, pendent above us, are our globes of light and heat. The universe is a magnificent

> " Cathedral boundless as our wonder,
> Whose quenchless lamps the sun and moon supply;
> Its choir the winds and waves, its organ thunder,
> Its dome the sky "

THE USEFUL AND BEAUTIFUL BLENDED.

The things which most directly minister to the support of our body are brilliant with beauty. While they sustain our life they also please our taste. The eyes of the farmer may expand with the greatest pleasure when he gazes upon the grain after it has been threshed from the stock, and as it lies upon his barn floor ready to be turned into flour to feed his household and put money in his pocket; but as it peeps above the

the Supreme Being."—Luthardt's *Moral Truths of Christianity*, p. 386.

earth in the spring, with its brilliant green, the richest and most soothing color upon which the eye can rest, its slender blades waving in the wind and reminding one of the gently-rolling waves with which old Ocean in his calmer moods is rippled, it forms a scene for angels to gaze upon with delight.   In the autumn the corn pours its wide and deep stream of wealth across the land; but when, through the summer months, it stands erect in its majesty, tinted with its golden colors, it is a sight on which the eye of heaven's Artist must look with an intensity of satisfaction.   The trees—especially when over their blossoms the changing blushes pass, signs of their coming fruitfulness—how like snowdrops they glitter with their pure beauty in the sunbeam!

It is not without significance that the sacred historian tells us that "out of the ground made the Lord God to grow every tree that is pleasant to the sight and good for food." Gen ii 9   The Almighty is no mere utilitarian.   He unites the beautiful with the necessary and useful   "What first meets the eye of the observer of the earth is the gorgeous carpet of grass which is spread over the larger part of its solid surfaee.   There are few objects more grateful to the sight than a lawn in early spring upon which the tender grass has attained just height enough to give it a uniform robe of green. The softness, the richness and purity, which we behold as the silvery light glimmers over it, completely satisfy the ideal of verdure. So when the crop has been removed, and the newly-mown meadow presents itself to view, with gladsome birds feeding themselves on the seeds and insects which can no longer be concealed, the passer-by is tempted to exclaim, How beautiful! If we would appreciate this matter of color, we have only to suppose that the grass and trees and plants had been red or yellow, and that a green thing were as rare in the gardens, fields and woods as a red or yellow thing is now. The eye rests with satisfaction on a field of golden wheat when it is ripe, interspersed in the landscape, but if grass, corn and leaves were of the same complexion, it would seek relief from the sight. So, too, were everything green—the sky, the water, and the ripe grain—the effect would be most ungrateful to the senses." * The variety of Nature is a part of its beauty.

The earth is beautiful. If we mount from

* *Biblical Repertory*, xxxv 666.

earth and look upon the heavens, the view expands into the sublime. There the useful and the beautiful are, in their highest degrees, inseparably blended. The arrangement which God has adopted to cause the sun to lighten, warm and render fruitful the earth, invests it and all its surroundings with the deepest splendor. The firmament in its robe of deep blue is gorgeously beautiful, while the sun majestically moves through it and has his burning light tempered by it. The clouds which ever and anon rise in it are beautiful; not merely when the bow spans them, showing in what grand water-colors the sun can paint on the dark background, and reminding us of the merciful covenant which God has made with man—that while the earth remaineth, seed-time and harvest, and cold and heat, and summer and winter, and day and night, shall not cease; but the drops of rain, every one worth its weight in gold to the ground, which gently fall from them and distill their fructifying influence through the soil, are things of beauty.

THE BEAUTIFUL WITHOUT APPARENT USE.

Moreover, God brightly paints his creation in ways which subserve no useful purpose in the merely physical sense of the word. Around our walls he throws most profusely his stereoscopic views to please and delight us. We cannot appropriate them to ourselves. We cannot turn them into food. The photographist can hardly catch their likeness, so evanescent are they. But they leave upon the mind an ennobling influence. " The glorious sunset is of no earthly use to us, otherwise than mere beauty and pleasure are in themselves of use. The gorgeous spectacle becomes at once degraded in our estimation by the very question of its possible utility. We love it, not for the benefit it confers, the use we can make of it, but for its sake, its own sweet beauty—because it is what it is. There it lies, penciled on the clouds, evanescent, momentarily changing. There it is, far off. You cannot reach it, cannot command its stay, have no wish to appropriate it to yourself, no desire to turn it to your own account or reap any benefit from it, other than the mere enjoyment; still, you admire it; still, it is beautiful." *

Often on an evening, when clouds that had overshadowed the earth through the day were breaking away and dispersing with the sunset,

* Haven's *Mental Philosophy*, p 277.

have I in the country, where a full sweep of the
heavens could be had, gone out to gaze upon the
gorgeous diorama.   I have stood entranced at the
scene of splendor: "That sky, that cloud, that
coloring, those tints that fade into each other and
change even as I behold them, those lines of fire
that lie in brilliant relief upon the darker background, as if some radiant angel had thrown aside
his robe of light as he flew, or had left his smile
upon the cloud as he passed through the golden
gates of Hesperus." *   I have been enraptured as
the beautiful expanded into the sublime; for the
sublime is the beautiful projected on a larger scale
and causing more intense and vivid emotions.†
When from this I have cast my eyes around the

* Haven, 267.

† Sir William Hamilton, however, contends that "the feeling
of pleasure in the sublime is essentially different from our feeling of pleasure in the beautiful.   The beautiful awakens the
mind to a soothing contemplation , the sublime rouses it to strong
emotion.   The beautiful attracts without repelling; whereas the
sublime at once does both, the beautiful affords us a feeling of
unmingled pleasure in the full and unimpeded activity of our
cognitive powers; whereas our feeling of sublimity is a mingled
one of pleasure and pain—of pleasure in the consciousness of the
strong energy, of pain in the consciousness that this energy is
vain."—*Metaphysics*, p. 628

whole heavens and brought them down to earth,
and surveyed the objects which were about my
feet, I have felt the words of the Psalmist, that
while honor and majesty are before the Lord in
his universe, strength and beauty are in this magnificent temple. Ps. xcvi. 6.   In view of its splendor, I have mounted to Him who conferred it all,
and have exclaimed, "How great is his goodness
and how great is his beauty who could, with so
liberal a hand, scatter these things through every
room and into every corner of his and our dwell-
ing-place!"   Then returning to my work, and feeling both the profit and the pleasure which such a
good and mighty Being can shed over our earthly employments, as well as over the works of his
hands, the ardent aspiration has gone forth from
my heart, "Let the beauty of the Lord our God
be upon us :* and establish thou the work of our
hands upon us; yea, the work of our hands,
establish thou it." Ps. xc. 17.

LEADS THE MIND TO GOD.

God has thus surrounded us with the beautiful
in the greatest profusion.   We have only to open

* "The beauty of the Lord, the loveliness, desirableness, all
that makes God an object of affection and desire to the believer "—
Dr. J A. Alexander on Ps. xxvii. 4

our eyes and we see it everywhere. Everywhere, too, if unintercepted, it leads the mind up
to its Author, and must have an important educational influence on the soul, not only for the
here, but for the hereafter, which the Most High
clothes in the garment of his own glory.* He
reveals himself through every work of his hand,

, * The beautiful, "the fringe of the garment of the Lord."—
Bailey. "I have sometimes thought that beauty is a gorgeous
robe spread over certain portions of the true and the good, to
recommend them to our regards and cluster our affections
around them."—*Dr. McCosh : The Scottish Philosophy*, p 297.
We may connect with this Augustine's doctrine of the beautiful,
"as consisting in that relation of the parts of a whole to each other
which constitutes its unity." Augustine made so much of *unity*
that he even analyzed pain into a feeling of the frustration of it.
In the field of philosophy Sir William Hamilton is an enthusi-
astic admirer of this great Christian writer. He refers to him in
one of his *Lectures on Metaphysics* (p. 98) as "the most philoso-
phical of the Christian Fathers," and in another (p. 412) as "not
only the most illustrious of the Christian Fathers, but one of the
profoundest thinkers of antiquity." Sir William, speaking of
the desire of unity as the second great tendency of our nature,
of which philosophy is the result, says (p 47), " Nor is it only
in science that the mind desiderates the one. We seek it
equally in works of art. A work of art is only deserving of the
name inasmuch as an idea of the work has preceded its execu-
tion, and inasmuch as it i itself a realization of the ideal model
in sensible forms."

in every dropping of his providence, in every variety and tint of beauty. As Thomson has poetized, it is the mark not of a true rational philosophy and science, but of a "*brute* unconscious gaze," to fail to recognize

> "The mighty Hand
> That, ever busy, wheels the silent spheres;
> Works in the secret deep; shoots, steaming, thence
> The fair profusion that o'erspreads the spring;
> Flings from the sun direct the flaming day;
> Feeds every creature; hurls the tempest forth;
> And, as on earth this grateful change revolves,
> With transport touches all the springs of life."

In the bitter and dead winter season the more winning forms of the beautiful disappear; but how musical are the words in which a poet has expressed God's manifestation of himself even in the tiny white messengers that flutter down upon us!—

> "Silently gentle, softly slow,
>   With buoyant fluttering,
> Flake upon flake, the feathery snow
>   Rests upon everything.
>
> "The rough strong branch, each twig and spray,
>   Smooth leaf of holly tree,
> Grass, hedgerow, housetop, busy way,
>   All white as white can be.

" How all God's doings manifold
   His power and wisdom teach '—
Sunshine and rain, and heat and cold,
   A loving-kindness each.

" And all this gently-falling snow
   Has symbol sweet to me—
How, without pause, his mercies flow,
   Silently, tenderly."

THE TASTE FOR THE BEAUTIFUL NATURAL.

Proceeding further, let it be observed God has given man, in the natural constitution of his mind, a taste for the beautiful in its various forms, and a sensibility in view of it—a faculty by which we recognize it and feel a peculiar emotion under it.*

* " Over against that beauty which the Creator has poured with lavish—I had almost said indifferent—hand over his creation, he has set a portion of man's nature whose function it is to drink it in; and as he never intended that this mere decoration of his works should engross the soul to the exclusion of the wisdom and goodness displayed in them, so he never intended that the sense for the Beautiful should absorb and destroy the sense for the True and the Good." I quote this from Dr. Shedd's *Essays and Discourses*, p. 58, for the purpose of emphasizing the latter part of it. The discourse from which it is taken, " On the True Nature of the Beautiful, and its Relation to Culture," is a powerful one. Its fundamental position is thus stated (p. 57): " It is indeed true that from eternity to eternity Beauty is a quality in the nature of the First Perfect and the First Fair, and from this

Philosophers have puzzled each other and wearied their readers in the discussion of the question as to what it is that constitutes the beautiful, and what the peculiar nature of the power by which the mind cognizes it. But in this they agree—that whether the beautiful be merely subjective and emotional, or something objective to the mind; whether it be merely a feeling in the mind, or something really existing out of the mind, but brought into contact with it, and through "the adaptation of our physical and mental constitution to the order and constitution of material things as they exist without," exercising its powers over it; whether, on the latter supposition, it lies in the novelty, or the utility, or the unity in variety, or the order and proportion,

---

fountain has welled up and poured over into the whole creation of God like sunset into the hemisphere; but it has been only as the accompaniment and adornment of higher and more august qualities. The Beautiful is not, as some teach, either the True or the Good; neither is it more absolute and perfect than these. These are the substance, the eternal essence, and it, *in relation to them*, is the accident. The Beautiful, indeed, inheres in the True and the Good, and it for ever accompanies them, even as light, according to the fine saying of Plato, is the shadow of God; but it is not, therefore, to be regarded as the highest of all ideas or as the crowning element in the universe."

of the things that we see, or (as I think is the
noblest explanation) in the exhibition by material
things of the spiritual ideas which underlie them,
the promptings and workings of the Infinite Spirit
by whom they have been created and fashioned
into shape and sent forth upon their mission to
actualize the eternal ideas of his mind, and which
we can perceive and sympathize with because he
has made us in his image,*—in this they agree,
that men instinctively perceive it and are possessed of a keen sensibility to it.   And the human
mind, without waiting for their learned discus-
sions, becomes entranced with the beautiful.   Before we can explain it we feel it.

"'All those,' says Dr. J. D. Morell, 'who
have shown a remarkable appreciation of form
and beauty date their first impressions from a
period lying far behind the existence of definite
ideas or verbal instruction.   The germs of all
their æsthetic impressions manifested themselves,
first of all, as a spontaneous feeling or instinct,

---

* Sir William Hamilton's definition, which certainly needs to
be further defined, is (*Metaphysics*, Lect. 46.), "that a thing
beautiful is one whose form occupies the imagination and understanding in a free and full, and consequently in an agreeable,
activity."

which from the earliest dawn of reason was awakened by the presentation of the phenomena which correspond objectively with it in the universe.' These primitive feelings exist in very different intensity in different individuals; and it is where they have most strongly manifested themselves at a very early period of life that we can see how fundamental a part of our nature they constitute, although they may be but faintly shadowed forth in a large part of mankind. They are peculiarly susceptible of development, however, by appropriate culture; under the influence of which they not merely grow up in the individual, but manifest themselves with increased vigor and more extended range in successive generations." *

The child enters but a little way upon the existence into which his birth has ushered him before his mind awakes to the contemplation of it. Hold up before him a flower, a bit of stained glass, any shining object, and how do his eyes glisten and his hands strive to secure it! Put the object within his grasp, and he hastily crushes it to pieces, not from any love of destruction, but, I suppose, in ignorance of what he is doing, think-

---

* Dr. Carpenter's *Mental Physiology*, § 188.

ing that he can more entirely secure the attraction.
If it were not for the total failure of recollection
in regard to the early period of existence which
marks our minds, we should probably have remembered, when we arived at an advanced age,
how we were struck with amazement on seeing
that acts which were but the natural promptings
of curiosity and of a desire to secure glittering
objects resulted in their ruin.*

How natural and independent of all education
it is Akenside has both poetically and philoso-
phically pictured:

> " Ask the swain
> Who journeys homeward from a summer day's
> Long labor, why, forgetful of his toils
> And due repose, he loiters to behold
> The sunshine gleaming, as through amber clouds,
> O'er all the western sky . full soon, I ween,
> His rude expression and untutored airs,
> Beyond the power of language, will unfold
> *The form of beauty smiling at the heart."*

As we grow in age the taste increases in its
manifestations. It exhibits itself in different ways,
Some minds will delight in what others look upon

* Dr. Noah Porter has, in his *Elements of Intellectual Science,*
an interesting chapter (vi.) on the " Development and Growth of
Sense-Perception " in infants.

with disgust. Education will give a symmetrical growth to the sensibility, and want of culture will dwarf and deform it. But the germ must originally have been in the mind, otherwise the differences could not exist. The savage possesses it as really, though not in a cultivated form, as the man of refinement who with delight frequents an academy of fine arts. He will stand entranced with admiration before the rushing waterfall as in the rays of the sun it reflects the varied colors of the rainbow; and beneath the splendor of the autumn sunset he will think with awe of the Great Spirit who resides behind it and lights it up with his glorious face.* To persons who, by a long life of vice, have familiarized themselves with the odious things of sin, and cut themselves off from the influence of the beautiful, there come times when their better nature speaks out and a tender association reopens their mind to the gentle influence. One of the most effective of the subor-

---

* Prof. Upham (in his *Elements of Mental Philosophy*, ii. 51) suggests that what among savages is to us repulsive really flows from the natural taste for the beautiful, though untrained. " Seeing how beautiful the fish of their lakes and rivers, the bird of their forests, and the forest tree itself, are rendered by colors, they commit the mistake of attempting to render their own bodies more beautiful by artificial hues."

dinate modes of reformation from vice is the
bringing of the debased soul back to a natural
and warm contact with God's works. For man
himself' is the crowning beauty of creation.
"The air-vault beneath which our globe revolves,
the deep restless sea, the giant mountain, the
flowing river, the impenetrable forest and the
trackless desert, independent of all animation,
present a spectacle of unrivaled grandeur and
sublimity." But it was when man was placed
over the whole that the work of creation was
very good and very beautiful. "What a piece of
work is a man! How noble in reason! how infinite in faculties! in form and moving how express
and admirable! in action how like an angel! in
apprehension how like a god! the beauty of the
world! the paragon of animals!" As he is a
microcosm of God's creation, whatever theory of
the beautiful may be adopted will find its ex-
emplification in him. And the contact with the
beautiful in Nature should help to recall him to
himself.*

* It was a very expressive tribute to the moral power of the
beautiful and of childhood which was paid by an uneducated
working-woman who was visiting an art-collection. As she was
looking upon one of the finest of the paintings of Jesus in the
arms of his Mother, she was heard to exclaim, "Who would

Thus wide as the universe is the beautiful—
wide as man is the taste for it. Moreover, the
gratification of this taste, the springing up of
the emotions which are connected with it, do
not depend upon the possession of its objects.
This is an idea that is worth signalizing, for it
shows how happiness is freer, richer, wider, than
wealth and possession.

A man may own beautiful objects and shut
them up from public view, and permit himself
alone to look upon them; but once let them be
exposed, and the beauty belongs not to him: it
is the property of every beholder.

The great objects of beauty are within the
range of all. The man of wealth may cover his
walls with the masterpieces of art. His favorite
visitors only may feast upon them, and they may
feel the pleasant sensations of the beautiful, and
therefore become really possessed of it more
intensely than the host and owner. But the
attractive works of God's creation are generally
as much within the range of the poor man who
has his liberty to look around him as of the rich
man who counts his money by the millions.

not try to be a good woman who had such a child as that?"—
Carpenter's *Mental Physiology*, p. 514.

THE ADAPTATION BETWEEN OUR MINDS AND THE UNIVERSE.

In establishing this adaptation between our minds and the external world, God designed that we should improve the power with which he has invested us, and enjoy its exercise. The wise Economist of the universe has not bestowed upon us any faculty with the intention that it should lie waste. If he has made the earth and the sky and the furniture thereof so beautiful, and if he has given us the faculty to see the beauty and have pleasure in it, he must have intended that we should seek and receive the happiness that is stored up therein. It is as really our duty to cultivate this taste as it is to cultivate those powers of the mind which have to do with what the German metaphysicians call "the bread-and-butter sciences," though *they* may be absolutely necessary for bodily support, while *this* is only highly improving and beneficial.

THE TENDENCY TO NEGLECT THE CULTIVATION.

In the active discharge of life's duties, however, the danger is great of largely overlooking this. Existence is made too much a hard, matter-of-fact thing. There are men who are literally encompassed by the beauties of the heavens and the earth, but who plod along their dull and dreary way comparatively unaffected by them. Tied hand and foot by the desire to secure the means of subsistence and to add to their money their lands and their houses, they neglect the cultivation of their finer feelings. There are farmers who, as they plough their fields or harvest their grain, have only to lift their eyes that they may behold the most gorgeous of scenes, or to cast them down at some object which their ·plough turns up or their reaper lays bare that they may see some of the most minutely beautiful of God's works; and yet they either hasten on without notice or simply glance at the sight, and soon drown its influence in the click of their machine : it does not immediately pay ; it is food and money that they are after—different in this from the peasant-poet of Scotland, who, as he once turned down a mountain-daisy with his plough, rested for a moment on his instrument, and, while he gazed with thoughtfulness upon the little thing, conceived the idea of that touching piece which begins with the soliloquizing regretful address :

" Wee, modest, crimson-tipped flower,
Thou'st met me in an evil hour,
For I maun crush amang the stour
    Thy slender stem :
To spare thee now is past my power,
    Thou bonnie gem ;"

And ends with the mournful moralizing,

" Even thou that mourn'st the daisy's fate,
That fate is thine no distant date :
Stern ruin's ploughshare drives elate
    Full on thy bloom,
Till crush'd beneath the furrow's weight
    Shall be thy doom."

There are business-men who toil along in their offices or counting-rooms, hastily swallowing their meals, and swiftly rushing through the crowded streets in pursuit of the wealth which they desire to pour into their coffers like a wildly rushing stream. Their brows furrow with care; their souls become dyed in the beggarly elements of the world; and while they are securing the coveted wealth, the rich beauty which God has placed within their grasp attracts no attention from them. Sometimes they think of a future day in middle or old age, when, having secured a competency, they will retire from business.

The prospect of a charming country place, amid green fields and bright flowers, tastefully laid out and furnished with all the ornaments that money can purchase, and enlivened by the cheerful ring of their children's laugh, steals in upon their minds in the heat of the day or during some of the wakeful hours of the night. But now they will attend only to business, so as to be the better able to secure and lay out that Alhambra, while they neglect the cultivation of the beautiful, as it might be done even in the midst of the most zealous and proper pursuit of business. They forget that, with the years, they and their children are changing. They are forming habits which, after a while, scarcely any effort of the will can break. A few years will place them beyond the power of enjoying what they vaguely anticipate. Better, far better, to prosecute business now in such a way as to enjoy God's gifts in connection with it, and actively employ them and all their powers in his service; better to make some spare hours for communion with his works, the contemplation of his heavenly and earthly attractions, and the delightful study of the world's best works of literature and art; better to throw around the evening circle now the

charm of their cheerful presence, by conversation and reading elevating the mind and bringing it into communion with the higher intelligences.

THE BEAUTIFUL CONSECRATED IN CHRISTIANITY.

Further, God has especially consecrated the
beautiful and made it a part of our religion.
Christianity itself is most beautiful. The Christian character in its symmetry is an object of
admiration. The Bible glitters all the way
through its supernatural manifestation of grace.*
No writers show a more exquisite taste, or give
a grander play to the imagination, or more gracefully press into their service the beauties of
Nature in the forms which they adopt to present
the eternal and infallible truth. Then the great
Teacher himself—how watchful was his eye ever
to catch up and set in connection with holy
things the most beautiful gems that he could
find! Himself "the Branch of the Lord, beautiful and glorious," his large heart sympathized
with Nature in all its forms and utterances; and

---

* "The dignity of religion requires that the sensible garment
in which truth is clothed should exhibit the form of beau'y."—
Luthardt's *Moral Truths of Christianity*, p. 228.

while he was engaged in the great work of redemption, delivering us from sin and curing the afflicted that met him in his daily path, he often stopped by the wayside, or on the sea-shore or the mountain-top, to feast his eyes with the enchanting scenes of the Holy Land, and to bring the minds of his untutored disciples into harmony with them.

JESUS A BEAUTIFUL PERSON.

I believe that even in the physical form of our Redeemer the highest type of the beauty of humanity was exhibited * He was *the* represen-

* This touches on an old controverted question. It is one of the unique peculiarities of Holy Writ that it gives no description of our Redeemer's form, and no hints from which a picture of him can be drawn. Nor do the church writers immediately succeeding the apostles venture to draw any Strange to say, no tradition settled the matter. Eusebius and Augustine complain that nothing was known about it. So near the Redeemer's own time, as within a hundred years of his death, a long controversy arose on the point. Isa lii 14 and liii 2 were claimed, on the one hand, as strictly declaring the absence of physical comeliness and beauty from his frame; on the other hand, Ps. xlv 2 was considered as settling that physically he was the fairest of men. Justin Martyr, Tertullian and Cyril contended for the former view, Cyril even declaring that Jesus was "the ugliest of the sons of men" Ambrose and Jerome declared that he was the

tative man : the perfection of human nature as the
Almighty created it in Adam, as it would have

most beautiful of mankind.   A letter represented to be from
Publius Lentulus to the Roman Senate, but which dates no
farther back than the eleventh century, giving a most charming
description of him, has been very widely published.   Another,
not so well known, is found in Epiphanius, who belongs to the
early part of the fourth century.   I copy it as a pleasant curiosity:
" My Christ and God was exceedingly beautiful in countenance.
His stature was fully developed, his height being six feet.   He
had auburn hair, quite abundant and flowing down mostly over
his whole person.   His eyebrows were black, and not highly
arched; his eyes brown and bright.   He had a family likeness,
in his fine eyes, prominent nose and good color, to his ancestor
David, who is said to have had beautiful eyes and a ruddy complexion.   He wore his hair long, for a razor never touched it;
nor was it cut by any person except by his mother in his childhood.   His neck inclined forward a little, so that the posture of
his body was not too upright or stiff.   His face was full, but not
quite so round as his mother's; tinged with sufficient color to
make it handsome and natural; mild in expression, like the
blandness in the above description of his mother, whose features
his own strongly resembled."   Farrar, in his *Life of Christ*, vol. i.
pp. 148 and 312, presents some of the arguments which sustain the
view I take; and (in ii. 463) he gives the *Lentulus* word-painting.
Ellicott, in his remarkably reverential and, especially in his copi-
ously strewn notes, critical *Life of Christ*, throws out this suggestive remark : " One further touch completes the divine picture—' in favor with God and man'—perchance designed to
hint to us that the outward form corresponded to the inner devel-

been in Adam's descendants if the first father had not fallen, and as it shall be after the resurrection day and on the regenerate earth though transformed and purified from the lower flesh-and-blood elements that belong to this state. By the overshadowing influence of the Holy Spirit the child Jesus was produced and born in union with the person of the eternal Son of God; and such a shrine of divinity could not but have the divine beauty. Through all the stages of earthly life, with the limitations of humanity, but without any of the imperfections and the sins of the fallen race, he grew up in every respect, physical as well as spiritual, the type and model of our nature.

The forty-fifth Psalm is a poetic description of the Messiah, of his Church and of the everlasting marriage union of the two. In the eighth verse the Bridegroom is gloriously portrayed. His personal grace, his warlike prowess, his righteousness, his rich adornments, are, one after the other,

opment, that the fullness of heavenly wisdom dwelt in a shrine of outward perfection and beauty, and that the ancient tradition which assigned no form or comeliness to 'the fairest of the children of men' was but a narrow and unworthy application of the general terms of Isaiah's prophecy."—Pp. 91, 92.

with rapid touches of the pencil, limned before us. The first color of the portrait is this: "Thou art fairer than the children of men; grace is poured into thy lips; therefore God hath blessed thee for ever." The fairest of all the children of men! It must have been as true of his form as of the words that dropped from his lips.

The prophet Isaiah, it is true, foretelling him in his sacrificial character and amid the extremity of his sufferings, thus paints him: "As many were astonied * at thee; his visage was so marred more than any man, and his form more than the sons of men." "He hath no form nor comeliness; and when we shall see him there is no beauty that *we* should desire him. He is despised and rejected of men; a man of sorrows and acquainted with grief; and we hid as it were our faces from him; he was despised, and we esteemed him not." lii. 14; liii. 2, 3. That, however, was photographed by the prophet, with the unerring sunlight of anticipative revelation, from the scene of the judgment-hall and the cross, after the fearful scourgings that had cut into the divine beauty of the form, and from the point of view of the cruel multitude who looked upon

* Or "shocked."

him with their hopes of a political deliverer for ever blasted.

But through all that, and behind it, and before it, the eyes of the Jews among whom Jesus of Nazareth lived beheld in him a specimen of human grace and nobility such as the world never saw before or since. *The* man! Fairer than the children of men! Showing in perfection the plastic and moulding and coloring power of the almighty Sculptor in living forms! Babes of rare beauty have, through exposure and cruelty and vices into which they fell, lost all their attractiveness and grown up with faces whose portraits would show none of the graceful lines and features that were possessed in childhood But the divine beauty of the child Jesus was preserved in the man by the perfect freedom of his body from all undermining, harrowing, disfiguring influences. Born with the perfect germ of humanity in him, free from the influence of hereditary depravity, committing no actual sin, he was never subject to any of the diseases which the Fall introduced as the sad heritage of the world, though he bare our sicknesses in the divine sympathy which made them his own. His healthy and strong body enshrined a so l which was the meet inmate of such a tabernacle, and which wrought itself in its own ethereal beauty on the physical frame and spoke through its expressive features.

How we should like to have seen that divinely favored body—the model human form! Free from all the personal and inherent effects of sin upon our race, no distorted feature marred the symmetry of its structure. No disease or sickness ever scarred or weakened it. Majestic dignity was in it blended with mild gentleness of demeanor. Over the manliness of its structure the glow of a divine expression, ever changing, yet ever the same, shed its glowing radiance;

"In his looks divine
The image of our glorious Maker shone."

But he now wears in heaven the same body, though of a more transcendent beauty still, the equal of which the hand of sculptor has never chiseled, the imagination of poet has never conceived and embodied in verse. And similar glorious forms his people are also to have. Here the bodies of some of them may be sadly marred by disease. They may never walk among the fair ones of the earth admired for their manly dignity or for their soft and delicate beauty. The eye may be closed, and its darkness never be dispelled by the light of heaven; or the ear may be stopped, and its stillness be unbroken by affection's tones; or the tongue may be tied, and never thrill with the tender emotions of the heart. But all shall be changed. Every eye shall see, every ear shall hear, every tongue shall join in the eternal song. Every redeemed form shall be perfect. No defect, no infirmity, shall pass through the grave. Sown in corruption, it shall be raised in incorruption; sown in dishonor, raised in glory; sown in weakness, raised in power; sown a natural body, raised a spiritual body. The spiritual body of the glorified shall have life in its highest, purest, most beautiful form, for it shall be fashioned like unto the glorious body of their Redeemer.

AN ADMIRER OF IT IN NATURE.

What Jesus possessed in himself he admired wherever he met it in the inanimate or animate, irrational or rational, creation around him. The contemplation of it was a source of happiness to himself; and a delicious training for those who were privileged to saunter with him over the hills

23

and the valleys of Palestine, as it still is for those who, guided by the inspired word-pencils, walk with him in a sanctified imagination's realm.

"Those of his followers in Judea who knew of his habitual retirement to the mountains for prayer, his temptation in the desert of the Dead Sea, his sermon on the hills of Capernaum, his transfiguration on the crest of Tabor, and his evening and morning walks over Olivet for the four or five days preceding his crucifixion, were not likely to look with irreverent or unloving eyes upon the blue hills that girded their golden horizon or drew down upon them the mysterious clouds from the depths of the darker heaven." Nor is it possible now for a properly disciplined Christian "to walk across so much as a rood of the natural earth, with mind unagitated and rightly poised, without receiving strength and hope from some stone, flower, leaf or sound, nor without a sense of a dew falling upon him out of the sky." *

* Ruskin, quoted in Peter Bayne's *Testimony of Christ to Christianity*, pp. 132, 133. Mr. Bayne introduces the quotation with these remarks (p. 131): " There is one other characteristic of Christ to be classed exclusively neither with the intellectual nor the moral powers, but tempering and beautifying both, which I must in no wise omit—his habit of dwelling affectionately on the aspects of Nature In modern times we have seen admiration

GRACE INTENSIFIES THE TASTE.

The legitimate influence of grace in the heart is, by its reflex power, to superadd an attractiveness to material Nature. Cowper, in his tender filial tone, has thus described the Christian :

> " He looks abroad into the varied field
> Of Nature, and though poor, perhaps, compared
> With those whose mansions glitter in his sight,
> Calls the delightful scenery all his own.
> His are the mountains, and the valleys his,
> And the resplendent rivers—his to enjoy
> With a propriety that none can feel
> But who, with filial confidence inspired,
> Can lift to heaven an unpresumptuous eye,
> And smiling say, My Father made them all."

for the beauties and sublimities of natural scenery become a passion, and it may well be doubted whether, in fiery intensity and absorbing degree, it is always the symptom of a strong, balanced or healthy mind. But in right quality and just measure it is, perhaps, a surer proof of moral health and intellectual completeness than any mental characteristic that could be named. It testifies to an openness to gentle, unexciting influences, to a freshness of soul rejoicing in Nature's dewdrops, to an innocence which can sympathize with the tender harmony of Nature's joy. It evinces a delicacy of soul that would recoil with sensitive pain from guile, from malignity, from baseness. It may fairly be doubted whether any man retaining the child-love for green fields and morning flowers has ever been consciously and inveterately bad. In its noble form this love of Nature is eminently a trait of Christian times."

It was the powerful metaphysical mind of
Jonathan Edwards which thus declared the transforming and heightening influence upon the works
of Nature of the grace of God in the saving revelation of Jesus to him: " The appearance of
everything was altered; there seemed to be, as it
were, a calm, sweet cast or appearance of divine
glory in almost everything. God's excellency,
his wisdom, his purity and love, seemed to appear
in everything; in the sun, moon and stars, in the
clouds and blue sky; in the grass, flowers and
trees; in the water and all Nature; which used
greatly to fix my mind. I often used to sit and
view the moon for a long time, and in the day
spent much time in viewing the clouds and
sky, to behold the sweet glory of God in these
things; in the mean time singing forth, with a
low voice, my contemplations of the Creator and
Redeemer."

The Almighty " by his Spirit hath garnished the
heavens." When that same Spirit enters a soul
and garnishes it anew with his grace, the beauty
within and the beauty without should leap into
communion with each other, and the attractiveness of the external works should be heightened
and bathed in a deeper brilliancy by the reflection

of the hue of grace from the rejoicing heir of heaven.

Very powerful, too, under the divine influence, is the devotion of strong and cultivated minds to God as the "First Fair." Thus wrote Augustine, in terms which might have been thought overdrawn and sentimental if they had come from a weaker intellect: " What do I love, when I love thee, Lord? Not the beauty of bodies, nor the fair harmony of time, nor the brightness of the light so gladsome to our eyes, nor sweet melodies of varied songs, nor the fragrant smell of flowers and ointments and spices—not manna and honey, not limbs acceptable to the embracements of flesh. None of these do I love when I love my God; and yet I love a kind of light, a kind of melody, a kind of fragrance, a kind of meat, and a kind of embracement when I love my God— the light, the melody, the fragrance, the meat, the embracement of the inner man; where there shineth unto my soul what space cannot contain, and there soundeth what time beareth not away, and there smelleth what breathing disperseth not, and there tasteth what eating diminisheth not, and there clingeth what satiety divorceth not. This is it which I love when I love my God." *

CHRIST'S ÆSTHETIC MORALIZINGS.

Especially did our Redeemer use Nature's scenes for the instruction of his followers, while amid the beauties that encompassed him, he the more enjoyed soul-communion with the Father.

"No moralist has excelled Christ in lessons of wisdom derived from Nature, and no poet has surpassed him in delicacy of perception for the beauty of flowers, the waters, the sky, and for the traits and habits of sentient creatures; and therefore it is foreign to the genius of Christianity to disparage a taste for the beautiful in the physical creation, or to undervalue this as tributary to the religious sentiment." †

* *Confessions,* book x. ch. vi 8.

† Dr. J. P. Thompson's *Theology of Christ,* p. 101. But against those who would antagonize Nature and Nature-worship to our religion, I would emphasize the protest with which Dr. Thompson accompanies the words that I have quoted: "The spirituality of worship must be distinguished from mere sentimentality in religion. The poetry of Byron abounds in apostrophes to Nature in the vein of worship. Novelists of the worst school of French license will pause in a tale of infamy to utter some pious feeling touching the stars, the trees, the flowers—to

Herein, too many of the Reformers fell into a serious error. In their zeal against Rome's corruptions and against the predominance of the sensible in its worship, they went to the other extreme—not of a too refined spirituality, but of too bare and repulsive surroundings of the spiritual. Our religion itself should prompt us not merely to enjoy the beautiful in Nature, but to cultivate it in our houses and in our churches, so as to render them fit places for the worship of Him who dwells in the "beauty of holiness," and for

invoke the sea, the breeze, the mountain, the cloud, the moon— Nature in whole or in detail—as the personification of the religious sentiment; and after this ebullition of devotion will proceed to deform virtue and to glorify vice. Confucius teaches that by meditating in the seclusion of the mountains and waterfalls man returns to the primitive goodness of his nature, and thus the magnificent growth of the forests and the delicate beauties of the garden become moral tonics to the soul. But that enthusiasm for Nature which never speaks the name of God, which expends itself upon effects without thought of the First Cause of all, which even substitutes an effect for the cause as an object of religious emotion, has no one element in common with the spiritual devotion that Christ declared to be the only true worship. It is at best but a more refined idolatry, reproducing in the mysticism of the pantheist and the dream-talk of the poet, the homage of the ancient Greek and Roman, or of the modern Hindoo and Chinaman, to material forms as representing some beneficent property or power in Nature."

the homes of those whose souls are beautified by
divine grace.

We cannot make the house of God and its atmosphere—our sermons, our prayers, our music, all
our surroundings—too beautiful to be in the spirit
of our holy religion ; beautiful in the true sense of
the word—not with a beauty of a meretricious, a
gaudy, an extravagant kind, but in imitation of
Nature itself.

Jesus lived as our example. His life was a
revelation upon earth of the heavenly life, and a
model of the course over which we should walk
to the glorious land. In this æsthetic element,
therefore, we should seek, as a part of our alle-
giance to him, to breathe his spirit, to be educated by his words, and to copy his habit. It is
a way, too, in which we may wonderfully increase
our happiness; for "to see, and in seeing to
converse with, all forms of grace and grandeur, is
to have the life multiplied a million times, and it
is to stretch existence and enjoyment to the
height and width of the universe." *

ITS ELEVATING INFLUENCE.

The make of our minds, the divine example,
the increase of our happiness, the consecrating

* Taylor's *Physical Theory*, p. 110.

power of our religion, thus call upon us to
submit our souls to the influence of God's beau-
teous works. If we will live in contact with them
in the devout spirit of children who remember
that their Father made them all, an ethereal influence will come in upon us; our hearts shall
expand; an atmosphere of pleasantness, of delight,
of comfort, will diffuse itself through our family
circles ; we shall find ourselves becoming richer
in true knowledge, quickened in pure and heavenly affections, opening our eyes upon a new world,
walking under an ampler heaven and breathing a
diviner air; we shall rise above earthly things
and burst forth into the admiring exclamation,
" O Lord, how manifold are thy works! In wisdom hast thou made them all : the earth is full of
thy riches." Ps. civ 24.

God has scattered them around us for this purpose. The mind is as really benefited by them
as the body is by its food or the intellect by its
readings. The man who passes along his busy
life, without stopping to gaze and feast upon
Nature's beautiful scenes and Art's imaginative
imitations, robs himself of an important part of
his birthright. He may live. He may be useful.
He may serve his God But there is a fountain

in his heart that has never been opened, and he becomes but imperfectly educated here for the majestic grandeur of the heavenly temple, ana for the magnificent choral service with which its spangled arches are for ever vocal.*

Heaven is resplendent with beauty. As revealed in the Bible, its pearly gates, its golden streets, its pure river, its tree of life brilliant with its monthly fruit, all reflecting the throne of God and of the Lamb, and giving light like unto a stone most precious, even like a jasper stone, clear as crystal, appear to us quenching the light of the twinkling orbs and the burning splendor of the

---

* Addison concludes his beautiful series of papers in the *Spectator* on the " Pleasures of the Imagination" (which perhaps are not read as much as they once were, and as they should still be) with a paragraph on the " infinite advantage this faculty gives an almighty Being over the soul of man, and how great a measure of happiness or misery we are capable of receiving from the imagination only;" which suggests the important part that the use or abuse of this power may have in preparing us for the future: "He can transport the imagination with such beautiful and glorious visions as cannot possibly enter into our present conceptions, or haunt it with such ghastly spectres and apparitions as would make us hope for annihilation and think existence no better than a curse. In short, he can so exquisitely ravish or torture the soul through this single faculty as might suffice to make up the whole heaven or hell of any finite being."

20

noonday sun. No night intervenes to break the
continuity of the glorious prospect. No wildly-
raging storms rush across it to dash in pieces any
of its fair objects. The beauty of holiness has its
dwelling-place there. The curse of sin, the only
odious thing that has crept into the works of God's
hand, and the source of all that is disgusting,
enters not. Thorns and weeds disfigure not the
ground. No dread portents fill the air and cause
men to crouch with fear. No horrid imprecations
are heard, no abominable acts of wickedness are
seen. In that temple of magnificence, round the
throne and shining in the image of God, stand the
glorified inhabitants, from whom, made altogether
beautiful by the perfecting influence of God's
grace, and therefore in harmony with the whole
scene, there goes up to Him who " is the sum and
substance, the beginning and the ending of all
truth, of all power, of all goodness, of all beauty,"
one enrapturing anthem: " Blessing, and glory,
and wisdom, and thanksgiving, and honor, and
power, and might, be unto our God for ever and
ever! Amen." Rev. vii. 12.

Is that our high calling? May we hope to be
among the citizens of that beautiful land and par-
ticipants in that scene of glory? Will we not,

then, so live that when our eyes close upon this world of sin and our spirits are transported beyond the Jordan of death, we shall not be dazzled by that shining splendor, as we are here when we pass suddenly from darkness to light, but shall have been prepared for it through the training that we have received in the loving, reverent, adoring contemplation of the beauty of the Lord in Nature and in grace? From a life of faith in Jesus we shall certainly enter heaven. But it will be through the union of the obedience of faith with the improvement of all our faculties and the loving use of all God's gifts, as we are favored with them, that our education will be rendered more complete, and our souls be brought into harmony with everything that shall greet us there.

Blessed, unspeakably blessed, are they who, washed in the blood of the Lamb, and fully prepared for the matchless brilliancy of the eternal city, sweep through the pearly gate and up the golden street to the immediate presence of the All-Beautiful, Good and True.

THE END.

www.ingramcontent.com/pod-product-compliance
Lightning Source LLC
LaVergne TN
LVHW011703060325
805301LV00003BA/46